TEACHING COMPUTERS IN PRE-K THROUGH 8TH GRADE

TEACHING COMPUTERS IN PRE-K THROUGH 8TH GRADE

ONE NEW TEACHER'S VOYAGE IN EDUCATION

Salvatore Mamone

iUniverse, Inc.

New York Lincoln Shanghai

Teaching Computers in Pre-K through 8th Grade
One New Teacher's Voyage in Education

iUniverse books may be ordered through booksellers or by contacting:

iUniverse
2021 Pine Lake Road, Suite 100
Lincoln, NE 68512
www.iuniverse.com
1-800-Authors (1-800-288-4677)

ISBN-13: 978-0-595-42436-8 (pbk)
ISBN-13: 978-0-595-86771-4 (ebk)
ISBN-10: 0-595-42436-8 (pbk)
ISBN-10: 0-595-86771-5 (ebk)

Printed in the United States of America

CONTENTS

LIST OF FIGURES

PREFACE

This book has been written to describe one new teacher's experience in teaching computers. This book has also been written to give insight to other teachers on how to teach computer use to pre-k through 8th grade. At first, it may seem impossible for any one person to teach all these grades but I have done just that at a private school in New York State. Moreover, in my first year as a teacher! How this came about will be discussed below and in the introduction. Before we discuss the issues involved in teaching these grades, it might be interesting if I describe my prior involvement with the teaching profession and the computer field and why I think that I might have the qualifications to write this book.

To start, I have been in the computer field for over forty years and I have held just about every position in this profession, from junior programmer to corporate network manager. I have also taught for over twelve years at three different colleges. I became a teacher in elementary school after I was laid off from a technical management position at a large telecommunications firm. After searching for over eight months and being unsuccessful in finding a new position in my field I decided to go back to my first love, teaching. I knew when I made this decision that it would be difficult. I knew that I would be unable to teach in New York City because I did not have my teaching certification so my only choice was to teach, per-diem, at a private school. This would give me the experience I needed to see if teaching would be what I wanted to do for the rest of my life. I knew from speaking with other teachers that teaching would be the hardest thing I ever did, which is what I expected. I had previously taught for over 12 years in three different colleges. During that time, I taught introduction courses as well as advanced topics such as *Data Structures and Algorithms*. Teaching in college is easy; as a college professor all you need to do is hand out the course syllabus, teach the lessons, and then let the students do the work. If they complete the assignments correctly and on time they pass, if not they fail. Simple. This is not how it works in grade school. In grade school, there is more class management and baby-sitting as well as teaching. You need to be able to get the students to learn and get along with each other and sometimes these things conflict. As with all other professions, there is a lot of politics involved in teaching. I quickly discovered how a principal is like a captain on a ship. A principal is absolute ruler.

You may not and should not disagree with the principal. It was just like being in an office again, but without the water cooler and salary.

I also discovered that it was much more difficult to create lessons for students at this level than for college students. You need to be much more creative in the early grades to hold the students attention and to get them interested in the topic. College students on the other hand are expected to do the research and work themselves. This book will contain many of the lessons and assignments that I created for my students.

I spent a lot of time deciding whether I should include my basic teaching experiences in this book, that is, what experiences did I have as a new teacher. I finally decided that you, the reader, might enjoy seeing the troubles that a new teacher had learning to teach. It might make you remember when you were a new teacher and make you glad that you no longer have to learn the ropes. It may also give you a laugh at my expense.

INTRODUCTION

Teaching computers in all grades; from pre-k though 8th grade sounds like the follow-up to the horror movie the *Blair Witch Project*, only this story is true. How in the world do you teach computers to all those grades? The answer is, very carefully. The experiences I had and the success (ok some failures) I had may be useful to you, the reader, in teaching computers. I hope it is because that is my reason for writing this book.

First, I want to make it clear that my experiences do not reflect on the students or the school where I taught. These are my experiences and they will certainly be different from yours. Second, I did not write this book to make money. After all, I am a teacher, why do I need money? The idea for this book came from my wife. Every evening I would come home and relay that day's trials to her and one day she suggested that my experiences might be useful or at least interesting to others. For her idea and for many other things I thank her.

This book is divided into sections. Each section will describe the experiences I had in a particular grade. In all class sections I have added examples of the assignments that I used in that particular class to facilitate learning. Later in the book, I added a section for web sites a teacher or student might want to visit. I know that these web sites may be out of date by the time this book is published, but then again, if the web sites are good they should still be available. I have included many of the typing and class assignments in a separate section identified by the grade for which the assignments should be used.

Because I was brand new to teaching in these grades, I encountered many experiences and difficulties that experienced teachers have had and have learned to deal with. I debated long and hard about putting these experiences in this book because most teachers do not need to read about a new teacher's troubles. On the other hand, I also felt that the reader might find it interesting to see that someone else had the same problems that they experienced. In the end, I decided to leave my experiences in this book. I hope you have a laugh at my expense and the experiences bring back fond memories to you.

At the end of this book, you will find a list of web sites that you and your students might find useful. I used some of the web sites to build my assignments and to research this book.

ISSUES

Because teaching in grade school was a new profession for me, I experienced numerous issues and problems that I had never experienced in the business world. Some of the problems were due to my inexperience and some were due to the environment. What follows is a brief discussion of some of these issues and my attempt at a resolution. I believe that I would have had a much easier time teaching if my principal was not new to the job. The combination of my inexperience and hers made the job more difficult for both of us. I also believe that the numerous changes instituted by the new principal confused the students and contributed to mine and the students problems.

Differences Among Pre-k Through Eight Grade

The differences in thought process, knowledge and social skills between pre-k and eight grades are extraordinary. Those in pre-k and K and to some extent first grade do not have the motor skills to type therefore how can you teach them? Those in 2nd and 3rd grade have the motor skills but what should they learn? Those in 4th and 5th grade need additional topics to keep class interesting. Those in 6th and 7th grade need advanced topics to prepare them for high school. Those in 8th grade are from another planet. All they are thinking about was that they were finally going to high school. All of the students need specific teaching based on their needs and skills. What follows later are a few topics that in general hold true for all the grades. In general, when I went through the trouble of creating an assignment I tried to use the same assignment for many of the classes. For example, if the assessment tests were to be completed in class by the 7th and 8th grade, the 5th and 6th grade students could use the assessment as a typing assignment and as a preview of what they could expect one day. This reuse of assignments was one way I could create enough lessons for the entire year.

Class Management

Managing a classroom full of students is demanding, adding a computer into the mix often complicates the process. Class management became one of the biggest problems I encountered in my first year of teaching. Most of the children felt that the computer lab was fun and should be treated like recess. They therefore became very noisy and out of control. Most of the time they wanted to sit with their friends and talk, especially the 8th grade students. In general, all the classes behaved this way. This problem came about because the prior teacher let the students play games most of the time in class. When I appeared, they expected the same. I did not feel that it was a good use of my time or their time to play games. I wanted them to learn and this came as a shock to most of the students. In some cases, I ran into continual hostility. Another problem I encountered was grading. The students had never been graded fairly before in computer class. That is, the students were given a grade (usually an A) but it was not really based on what they knew or did. This enhanced their idea that computer room was a fun period. Since I was new to teaching in these grades the issue of class management became my main priority especially since the new principal's office was near the computer lab and she constantly complained about the noise in class. Sometimes the noise was so bad that other teachers could hear the students. Fortunately, the other teachers knew that in the past computer class was noisy and therefore it did not annoy them.

In an attempt to gain control over this problem I asked other teachers in other schools what I should do. One suggestion was to assign students to specific seats to separate friends. This sounded like a good idea and I did try it with limited success. The first day students would take their assigned seats but then they would gravitate to be near their friends. I had to remind students constantly to return to their assigned seats. This situation did not work out well because I did not want to be a policeman. I am also considered an easy or laid-back teacher. I never yell or get angry. I am also a notoriously easy marker. In college, I can remember one particular midterm that I gave to an advanced class. I felt the exam covered what I had taught and reflected what I wanted the students to know. After handing back the grades one student wanted to know why I gave such an easy test. Of course, the rest of the class groaned and wanted to make him be quiet, but I gave an answer that I feel is true no matter what class you teach. I said, "If you paid attention in class and did the assignments, then the test would be easy."

Now, in order to get the class under control, I had to be more forceful in class. It was not what I wanted to do but I had no choice. I started to tell the students to be quiet, I shut the lights in the class, and I walked up to students to remind them. I tried so many different things to quiet the class. Most times the class would not pay attention, but sometimes they would. I would say this aspect of teaching is the most difficult, time consuming, and in general a large pain. I am not sure how other teachers can deal with this without pulling their hair out.

As far as grading, I eliminated that issue by giving grades for each day's assignment. Although I could not grade the students for real, at least not at first, the students did not know that. At first, I gave the grades to their official teacher and she used my input to determining the student's grade. Later I was allowed to give my own grade to the students. This allowed my input to become their official grade. This worked out very well because the other teachers knew that I was actually teaching and the students knew that they had to do the class assignments. Because the previous instructor gave the students a bogus grade, most students felt that they would get the usual A. Now the students would receive a grade that truly reflected their knowledge and participation in class. This encouraged the students to work harder and many of the students appreciated the new learning experience.

Male vs. Female Teacher

At the time I accepted this position I did not realize that I was the only male teacher on the staff. I am not sure how this affected the other teachers or the students, but as for me, it did not matter. Sometimes my presence did seem to make it uncomfortable to the female teachers. At faculty meetings, I know that they wanted to say things but they held back because I was there. Eventually I was no longer asked to attend the meetings. I am not sure if they felt uncomfortable with me at the meetings or if it was because I was a per-diem teacher. Personally, I believe that it was good for the students to see that it was all right for a man to be a teacher. I guess the way I teach could also help the students by giving them another perspective on things. My opinion always was that teaching is not a female profession any more than medicine is a male profession. When attending large professional meetings with teachers from other schools I noticed that at least 90 to 95% of the teachers were female. These conferences were the same as computer conferences that I have attended. They both consisted of free food and several one-hour technical sessions.

It would seem that at least in my geographic area, teaching is still a female profession. That is too bad because teaching, to me, is the most difficult but most rewarding thing I have ever done.

As far as I could tell, the students did not care that I was male although I noticed that some of the eight grade boys did want to talk about sports with me. They wanted to know if I played any sports in high school, what the teams were like in high school and other things based on my experience with high school. The girls just treated me as a teacher. I believe that my life experiences and how I presented topics in class gave the students a different look at the subject matter and was good for their education.

Bathroom

One unexpected issue that came up while teaching is the amount of times children need to go to the bathroom. This is especially true in the Pre-k and kindergarten classes and was something for which I was unprepared. Since I did not have an assistant in the kindergarten class, I had to let the students go to the bathroom by themselves. I never felt that this was safe or a good idea, but because I could not leave the classroom unattended I had no choice. This was not a problem with the older grades although I did notice that more students needed to get a drink or go to the bathroom or both when a difficult topic was to be discussed in class. I never questioned a student when they said they needed to go to the bathroom or get a drink. The last thing I needed was for a young student to have an accident in my class. In general, I would only allow one student at a time to leave the room. This was to prevent students congregating in the hall and making noise. I never had a problem using this technique in any of my classes until I was told that no one was permitted to leave the room. Students were given assigned times when they could go to the bathroom or to get a drink. They were not permitted out of the room at any other time. By using this guideline, I was better able to manage this aspect of the classroom.

Supplies to Have On Hand

Most teachers, through experience, learn what supplies to have on hand. I discovered quickly what I needed in the computer room. Besides pencils, paper, and normal supplies that every teacher should have in his classroom I discovered that I needed special supplies at this school. It did not take me long to figure out what supplies I needed to have on hand. I soon discovered that I had better have tissues on hand for runny noses and for when the young students get too rough with each other and cry. When the students did get too rough I comforted the one crying and sent the other student to the principals office, where they would remain for the rest of the period.

I also kept a supply of soft candy on hand for comfort and to perk students up. Sometimes a small piece of candy would make all the difference when a young child is having a difficult day. The bad thing about having candy in your desk is that the temptation to eat it yourself is great. Before long, the candy would run out and after several bags of temptation, I finally stopped bringing candy to school.

Another supply I kept on hand was something to give students when it was their birthday. Sometimes, on their birthday, a student would go to each teacher and say it was his or her birthday. The teacher then added something to the student's gifts. I had a small supply of things like pencils and useful things to give them on just these occasions. As with most teachers, I was never reimbursed for any supplies that I bought for the class.

Grading Structure

I have been grading students in college for many years. As noted, I am a notoriously easy grader. In college, you needed to go out of your way to fail my course. I would work with a student to make sure they passed.

In elementary school, I tried to be just as easy a grader but it was difficult. There was just too big a disparity between the ability of the student's. In some cases, students were so good that they got an A+, in other cases students were so bad that giving them a C was hard to do. In general, I would be as generous as possible. If a student did all the assignments during a semester, they would pass the course with at least a C. If they missed one assignment, I would grade the remaining assignments but give them a lower average based on the missed assignment. If they missed more than one assignment, they would get an incomplete for their grade. The incomplete would signal a warning to the students, to the other teachers and to the student's parents that something was wrong. This method may not work for all subjects, schools, or grades but in general, it worked for me. This also brought a number of phone calls from parents wanting to know why their student received an incomplete. It just took one incomplete grade and a call from a parent to motivate the student to complete the next work assignment.

How often to grade is an issue with any class. To ensure the students had a change to get a good grade, I graded every assignment. The logic behind this method was, the more grades, the better the average would be. If I only graded three assignments during a semester, one poor grade could mean a poor mark for the semester, whereas if the student had ten assignments during the semester, one poor grade would not affect his average as much.

Another grading issue pertained to the Rubric grading structure. This was a method of grading that all teachers in my district were required to use. The Rubric system was a method of grading that ensured that all teachers graded the students the same. If you have never heard of this system, the following is a brief view on how it worked. After a student is given some form of test or assignment along with a set of instructions, the student would be graded. The instructions could be as simple as, *The written paragraphs must contain a beginning, middle and conclusion.* If the student completed the assignment using the required instructions, they could get the highest grade. If not, points were deducted. All teachers were required to grade by verifying that the students followed the instructions. If all teachers followed the same Rubric rules it is assumed that a student would be graded the same irrespective of the teacher doing the grading. The scoring Rubric ran from zero to five where a zero meant that the student did not use accurate data, failed to answer the question, the assignment was illegible or no sense could be made of the response, or the response is incoherent. A grade of a five was just the reverse, where the student answers all aspects of the task (does what the answer requires), uses accurate data, develops ideas that are logical. The other grades consist of some subset of the prior explanation. I did my best to adhere to these rules so that the students would be used to this type of grading and the other teachers would know what I was doing.

In order to keep track of my grades I created a rather comprehensive Excel spreadsheet of grades. Each grade (pre-k to 8th) was a separate workbook of several sheets. One sheet for the class would contain detailed information on the grade as well as complex formulas that I devised which created a term grade. The other sheets in a grades workbook contained a small subset of information that I gave to the homeroom teacher. This system worked very well because it was easy to maintain consistent grades throughout all classes.

The formulas that I created are much too complex to describe in this book and would probably not work in your class. I took the multiple grades (one for each assignment) for each semester, found the average, and then converted the average to a letter grade. I also included extra points for attendance and class participation. The formula would modify the grade average based on the number of completed assignments.

Disciple/Motivation

One way to try to gain control of a class is with specific and guided disciple. In my school that meant being sent to the principal's office. Being sent to the principal's office meant that you lost some special privileges and you could not be in the computer room or whatever classroom you came from. In general, this is a very distasteful practice. I finally had to use this practice because it became unbearable trying to keep the children as quiet as the principal expected. To be honest I do not know how you can keep a class like computer class quiet.

Students want to talk with their classmates and in many cases ask the other students for help. If it was up to me, I would not be afraid of this interaction. As with most things in life, it was not up to me.

Time out is another form of disciple that some teachers use. Time out is an enforced time alone used as a consequence of unwanted behavior. I sometimes used this technique with limited success. I would remove the student from his/her workstation and leave them to sit on a chair away from the class. This usually embarrassed the student but was less stressful than sending the student to the principal's office. Sometimes, especially with the early grades, this punishment became too hard on the students. I had incidents when the student being disciplined in this way would cry. Like most normal people there is no way that I can stand to see a child cry nor can I justify making a child cry, so I very soon gave up on this form of discipline.

Students, no matter what grade, need to be motivated. If they are not motivated, they probably will not learn and they can be disruptive in class. Many years ago, I wrote and published a paper, *Empirical Study of Motivation in a Entry Level Programming Course*, published March 1992 in IEEE SIGPLAN. This paper discussed motivation for students in an introduction computer class in college. The paper included information that I gained over many years of teaching at three colleges. What I found was that students who *wanted* to be in the class learned more and received a better grade than students who *had* to be in the class. This may not have any bearing in the prek-8 grades but it does show that students can do better if they are happy to be in the class.

Class Integration

A major objective that I initiated for my computer class early in the semester was to integrate computer topics with other topics such as English, math and history. The major reason was to give the students extra knowledge on their core subjects. Although it seems difficult to do, this process is much easier than it appears.

Just about everything that we do with a computer requires some English skills (Word, Word Perfect) or math skills (Excel, Lotus 123). By integrating these topics with my computer class, I was able to expand on what the students were learning in their other classes. This was important because the student's English skills, especially writing were so poor.

My first step in this integration was to ask the other teachers what they were teaching in their classes. For example, if the English teacher gave the students a book report to write, I would use that writing assignment as an assignment in word processing in my class. I would explain formatting and margins, etc in order for the students to type the report as required by their English teacher.

I integrated history in my computer class by introducing assignments based on the history of computers (hardware and software) and of the Internet. I also introduced several assignments on the history of robots and on the history of communications. All of these assignments will be found later in the assessment section of this book.

I integrated math by having the students use the built-in calculator and by given students Excel assignments. Some of the Excel and calculator assignments are shown later in this book.

I believe that this integration of computer class with the students other subjects was an aid to their education. It was helpful to them, the other teachers, and the school. It was helpful to them because I was reinforcing their knowledge in the other subjects as well as teaching them about computers. It was helpful to the teachers because the students were learning about the other subjects in a different way, thereby aiding their instructions. It was helpful to the school because I believe the students were receiving better grades in all their subjects. Several of the students, especially in grades six through eight, told me that they appreciated the way I was teaching because it was reinforcing what they were doing in their other classes.

THE CLASSROOM, THE COMPUTERS, AND COMPUTER SOFTWARE

This next section will deal with the class layout, the computers in the lab, and software that I used. Each section on software will discuss the pros and cons of the specific piece of software. Because Microsoft software is so common and it was supported by the school's vendor it became the software of choice at my school.

The Classroom

The classroom was setup so that usually each student would have their own computer during class. This was not always possible because there were nineteen machines and some classes had 20 to 22 students. This meant that two students sometimes had to share a machine. This was not always a problem but at times, it could be. When two students, who did not get along, had to share a machine I would need to discover that quickly so that I could separate them. This was another reason why I used assigned seats. Having more than one student at a computer could also be a good thing because they could interact and learn from each other. This did however tend to increase the noise level in class. In general, I decided not to have more than one student at a computer in order to maintain noise control. If necessary I would let one of the students use my computer to complete the class exercise.

Another issue I encountered was computer setup time. Most times one class would be over and then five minutes later the next class would start. This would happen if I was lucky and the teacher came back in time to pick up her students. When she was late, the other class would be outside waiting to get in. This allowed no time for me to setup the machine for the next class. This also increased the noise problem because the students were outside the room talking. I became very fast on installing CD's and setting up machines for the next class. To solve this problem I tried to end the class on time or a minute or two early.

One "solution" that I tried to overcome the noise issue was to install headsets on the computers. Headsets would allow students to interact with a machine and they could put the sound as loud as they could stand it. This seemed like a good attempt at noise control but it was not. The younger grades did not like using the headsets, they said the headsets "hurt", but they were the ones who I most wanted to use the headsets. The older students loved the headsets. They would bring in CD's, which they were not allowed to do, and play music to drown me out. This increased my setup time because now I had to put headsets in for the early grades and take them out for the later grades. I debated unplugging the speakers but this would require even more work on my part and would not eliminate the problem. In the end I let anyone who wanted to, use the headsets and I put the speakers and sound control very low.

Setup also included putting CD's in the machine for some grades. In order to facilitate learning, I used educational CD's for pre-k and kindergarten. This meant I needed time to insert the CD's and to start the programs before the students arrived. I also needed to take the CD's out and end the programs before the next class came in. This would not have been that big an issue except the grades did not come to lab in order. For example, on Friday I could have the seventh grade followed by pre-k followed by the eight grade. This created quite a logistic problem. There was no easy solution to this problem other than being faster on installing and removing CD's.

One additional problem involved the layout of the computer room. In my class, to save space, the computers were setup to face the wall (Figure 1). This arrangement allowed me to see the student's screens. Therefore, when I talked I was talking to the back of the student's heads. The students could not hear me and they could not tell if I was looking at them unless they turned completely around. I very much wanted to change the layout of the room and have the computers face me but because of the cost involved, this could not be accomplished. I almost asked if I could do the work myself, but since I did not have tenure at the time, I did not want to risk alienating anyone.

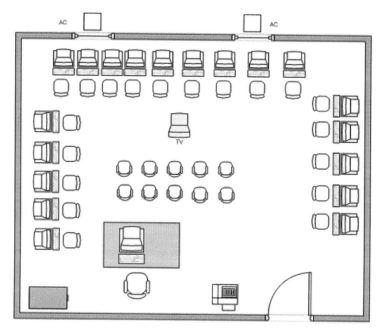

Figure 1—Computer Room Setup

I can recommend, as a setup for a computer room, that you place the computers facing the teacher so that the teacher does not teach to the back of the students head (Figure 2). My observation was that much of the noise and lack of attention could have been eliminated if the computers were setup in that way. Eventually I placed several rows of seats in the front of the class facing the TV that was attached to the teachers PC (Figure 1). The TV was on a shelf placed high enough for all the students to see. This allowed me to walk and face the students and explain the day's assignment without taking to the back of their heads.

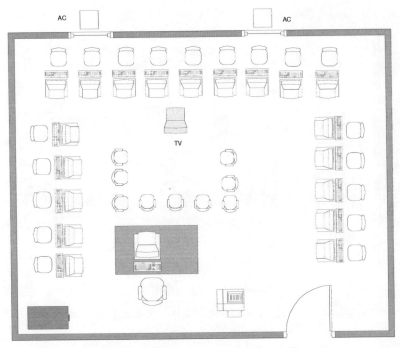

Figure 2—Suggested Computer Room Setup

Another issue with my computer room concerned the heat generated by the computers. The computer room tended to get very hot, even in winter. When I arrived in the morning, the room was cold because I had the maintenance people lower the thermostat. After turning on all the machines, the room quickly became warm. Because of the heat generated, I had to leave the air conditioning on whenever I taught a class, even in winter. I also needed to remember to turn the air conditioning off before leaving for the day or the room would be too cold the next day.

In order to safeguard the machines all computers were powered off at the end of the day and turned back on in the morning. This meant that I needed to be in class early to prepare the machines for the day, and I had to remain after the last class to shut the machines down. As most teachers will tell you, this work was necessary, unappreciated, and unpaid labor.

If you are involved in a computer room setup, you need to have a lot of experience and you need to take a lot of care to ensure the equipment is installed correctly and safely. If your school and district have the funds, you should consider wireless laptops for the installation (see Wireless Equipment, Hand-held and Laptops below). This would eliminate much of the wire clutter associated with a computer room. If you use laptops, you also need to consider security for the equipment. It is possible to generate security for the equipment because many companies sell laptop and associated storage cabinets in order for the equipment to be locked up safely after class. If you allow the students to take the laptops home to work on their homework, you must have some method of documenting what students have what equipment (serial numbers) and when. The student's parents must also be aware of this extra responsibility given to their children in order for the parents to help with securing their child's school laptop. If my school had laptops, I would not recommend the machines leave the school. The responsibility to the students and their parents and the possible legal and financial issues to the school were too great.

One alternative to self-installation and support is outsourcing. Outsourcing will allow schools the freedom to concentrate on teaching and have someone else manage the equipment. One of the many benefits to outsourcing is the associated support. If there is any problem with the equipment, the vender is responsible for the solution. The vender is also responsible for the software and any updates. Outsourcing is a good approach to the management of a computer lab in a school or district. Outsourcing is becoming so popular that many large companies now have their entire computer network outsourced. The school were I worked used an outsourcing firm for all their computer needs.

Wireless Equipment, Hand-held and Laptops

A growing number of schools are incorporating laptop computers and wireless Internet technology into their buildings and classrooms. Most U.S. public schools are equipped with desktop computers and computer labs, but the relatively new wireless Internet technology called Wi-Fi gives pupils instant access to the Internet to help with any subject in any classroom.

Wi-Fi is already available in many universities, which generally have more resources, but now the technology is trickling down into lower-level schools. It is one of the fastest-growing budget items for technology.

Over 90 percent of students attend the 110,000 public schools throughout the United States from kindergarten through 12th grade. These schools combined spend about $6.2 billion a year on technology needs, including hardware, software, networking equipment and staff development. Of that, about $500 million was spent on wireless technologies in the 2001-2002 school years, but that is expected to double in 2002-2003 and quadruple the following year.

Wi-Fi is an ultra high-speed wireless Internet connection usually available within a radius of a few hundred feet. By setting up multiple access points or "hot spots", schools can make wireless Internet access available throughout their school.

There are some benefits and drawbacks to installing a wireless network at your school. Some benefits include the following. Wireless computing makes possible a flexible configuration of classrooms, so that students can take with them whatever tools they need and use them wherever they happen to be. Because of the wireless connection, students can work outside at lunch or on break or anywhere. The work they perform can include greater depth and involve more critical thinking and research. Wireless networks are cheaper to install than wired connections, which are limited to areas with power outlets and other necessary equipment.

There are also some drawbacks to a wireless network. Some schools might be overwhelmed by the complexity of the technology and its rapid pace of change. Some teachers have also complained about greater distractions when students use their laptops to play games or surf the Web during class. Some teachers also object to seeing a sea of laptops and student faces down instead of looking at them. Some students have also noticed that their grades suffered as a result of too much e-mailing or instant messaging during class.

Laptops are now being used in many schools. Laptops are more expensive than desktop machines, although the prices are dropping; there are benefits to using laptops in computer class. If you have responsible students, laptops could be assigned to the students in order for them to do their work at home. In combination with a wireless network, laptops would allow students to do work in any classroom without having to wire each room. If you are considering laptops, you must also consider security for the machines. Can you allow the computers to leave the school after class? If you allow the machines to be taken out of class the school must have strict rules, in writing, on responsibilities for the machines. A document should also be signed by the parents informing them of their responsibility should something happen to the machine.

Some schools might want to consider handheld computers in the classroom. Many schools are experimenting with handheld's, such as Palm's as well as others. Handheld computers are small and do not have very much processing power or storage space, but they can be useful in some cases. With handhelds, students can devise new ways to improve their own learning, such as practice quizzes to beam to each other, and using handhelds to track assignments. Another result is students gain a level of responsibility by being responsible for the computer. Handhelds can be very effective when the class is large and there are not enough machines for each student. Handhelds are also less expensive than even used computers. Handhelds can also be disruptive in class as students beam messages to each other. The decision to use handhelds must also take the experience of the students in mind, and the level of security that you can assign to them.

IM or Instant Messaging

Instant messaging or IM is a form of real-time communications between two or more people via typed text. Popular instant messaging services on the Internet include: Windows Live Messenger, AOL Instant Messenger, Yahoo!Messenger, Skype, Google Talk, as well as many others. In contrast to e-mail or the phone, when you use IM you know whether the person you want to "talk" to is available. This is accomplished by the use of online status or away messages. The user also creates a private list of people that they want to converse with. When one of these people logs on this event is logged in the list. By examining this list it is easy to tell which people on the list are available to "talk" with at that given moment. Instant messaging is becoming more popular but its popularity may be surpassed by the use of text messaging on cell phones. Text Messaging is a similar technique that can be used with a cell phone, PDA or pager. Text messaging is used for short messages that are no longer than a few hundred characters. Because of this restriction people who send text messages usually use abbreviations. A typical abbreviation is PCM (please call me) or BBIAM (be back in a minute). Students with cell phones often send text messages in class. This can be a problem when they need to take a test because they often send the answers to each other. A list of abbreviations can be found at the on-line encyclopedia Webopedia www.webopedia. com/quick_ref/textmessageabbreviations.asp.

Installing Software

Installing software is an easy task and is just about intuitively obvious. Almost all purchased software will come with instructions for an easy install however, if you need to install software you should:

- Verify that the software is legal. Never install software that is not shrink-wrapped and purchased.
- Place the CD or DVD in the CD or DVD drive

- The next step will probably be a series of install steps. Use the defaults as marked. You must agree to the license agreement before the software will install.

If the install process does not start, choose RUN from the Start menu, and type D:\Setup. If your drive is not "D", type the appropriate letter.

Because you will probably be responsible for the software on the schools computers, it is very important that you follow the legal requirements for this software. Failure to follow the legal requirements may get you and your school in trouble. Companies that create software, whether educational or business related, have a financial stake in that software. You may not purchase one copy of a product and then install it on more than one computer. That is illegal, unless you have a site license for the software. Updates to install software follow this same procedure. If you have five copies of software you may not purchase one update and install it on five machines. If you have a copy of software, you may not install that one copy on a server and then allow the computers in the room access to the software. Even clip art, music, articles and similar topics have downloading restrictions from the Internet. You can check copyright ownership of information on the web sites, www.loc.gov or www.mpa.org. Some general copyright guidelines are:

- You may make backup or archival copies of your software disk for protection. You may not burn additional copies of software.
- If you have one copy of a software title, you may install that software on a server however, it can only be used on one networked computer at a time. The general rule is if you have *n* copies of a title then *n* computers may use the title at the same time but not more than *n* computers.
- In general, you may download pictures and information from commercial and non-commercial sites for students to access. You may not download copyrighted material without permission. You may not repost the information without permission from the owner.
- In general, you may download MP3 audio clips.
- You may not distribute purchased material over the web.
- You can use other people's intellectual property for educational purposes without permission. For example, School A tapes an interview of someone and posts that interview on their school web site. You may download that interview and use it in your class.
- Video tapes, such as movies, may be used in class for instructional purposes, but not as entertainment or as a reward.

Recently changes have been made to copyright law that affects software. To examine these changes on line, go to www.ala.org/washoff/teach.html.

The Technology, Education, and Copyright Harmonization Act (TEACH) was passed into law in 2003. This law allows schools transmit education content to students at any location (distance education), and expands the range of copyright-protected works that may be used for distance learning. For addition information visit the American Library Association's Web site at www.ala.org/washoff/teach.html.

The Internet

The Internet, "invented by Al Gore", is and will shape the way we live, work and shop. The Internet can be an important learning aid if access is available in your school. Because my private school was so small, we could not afford Internet access for our network. It is possible that by the time this book is published we will have access.

Internet access can be used to allow the students to research their assignments. Access can also be used to aid in the class discussion. The most important reason to have Internet access in the class is to enable the students to research their assignments.

Even though when I started to teach at this school the school did not have Internet access, I was still able to discuss the web with the students and why Internet access was important. A recent article in *Technology & Learning* magazine claimed that 80% of teachers had Internet access in their classrooms, which means that my school was not the only school without access. Of the 80%, 66% said that the Internet is not well integrated into their classroom. Fifty percent said that they use the Internet for less than 30 minutes a day. These numbers indicate that many schools have Internet access but do not know what to do with it!

One of the class assignments that I gave the class involved the web. I also attempted to have the students perform web development in class using HTML (Hypertext Markup Language) but this topic proved to be too difficult for the class to understand. Although we were unable to complete the assignment to build a school web site, we still used several periods to discuss the web and how it should and could be used. The web assignment is described at the end of the assignment section later in this book. The class web site assignment, shown later, was a practical assignment and was an exciting assignment for my class.

Access to the Internet can bring new problems such as restricting access. How much can you restrict access and what can students download? Legal requirements as well as civil rights can come into play when you add this important tool to your school. If your school has web access, you should consider a web filtering device or software. The software should include some reporting device that reports sites access, usage, and attempted access to unauthorized sites. Recent legal questions on restricting Internet access also need to be examined. If you wish to restrict access, you may use filtering software or hardware devices.

Some filtering software and hardware products include:

- SchoolMarshall by Marshall's Software (www.marshallsoftware.com).
- N2H2 sells a software plug-in that adds filtering to operating systems (www.n2h2.com).
- Net Nanny Software runs on individual computers not a server (www.netnammy.com).
- ScreenDoor by Palisade System allows administrators to set access rules (www.palisadesys.com).
- SmartFilter by Secure Computing contains lists of sites that schools can choose to block (www.securecomputing.com).
- Cyber Sentinel Network by Security Software Systems captures the screen of possibly objectionable material accessed by a student and then reports the activity to the administrator (www.securitysoft.com).
- SonicWALL's Pro 100 Education Edition is a security appliance that offers firewall, antivirus, content filtering and security management (www.sonicwall.com).
- iPrism by St. Bernard's is a filtering tool that monitors, blocks, and reports on Internet activity within schools (www.stbernard.com).
- SurfControl is a web filter that features advanced customization, user notification of blocked sites and the ability to block files that are virus-infected or take up too much bandwidth (www.surfcontrol.com).
- Symantec Web Security combines antivirus and Web filtering in one package (www.symantec.com).
- Vericept's VIEW Filter logs activity that falls outside rules set by the administrator (www.vericept.com).
- Websense Enterprise allows an administrator to set up Internet access by user, group, computer, or network (www.websense.com).

If your web site is accessible to outside people then you should include a firewall to prevent unauthorized access to your school web site. A firewall can be either software or hardware and is necessary for your school computers.

You should consider teaching your students about the Internet and how it can be used. You should also explain the limitations of the Internet. They should be made aware of several important facts. First, information that they find on the Internet does not have to be accurate. Just because you found it on the Internet does not make it true. Second, how current is the information. Current information may not be important, but for many topics it is very important. You and your students should try to obtain information from reputable web sites, some of which are listed later.

Another aspect of the Internet in the future will be the ability of schools to offer courses on-line. This type of education is called *Virtual Learning*. Many colleges are now offering entire degree programs on-line with very little interaction with other students. To me it appears that the students will miss many experiences if they attend school in this way. Teaching to the early grades should be performed in person. One important reason for face-to-face teaching is that young children need the interaction of their peers to develop. Another reason is the lack of feedback that students, especially in the early grades, need and would not receive with virtual learning.

Some schools might consider Virtual Learning because of the size of the school or the inability to attract quality teachers. Other reasons might include help for disabled students or additional education for honor students. If you are considering this form of education for your school be aware that the cost is usually too high for the software and equipment. You should also consider the impact this form of education will have on the students because of the lack of peer interaction and lack of teacher feedback.

Some virtual learning providers include:

- Connections Academy www.connectionsacademy.com, grades k-12
- K12 www.k12.com, grades k-12
- Virtual High School www.govhs.org
- Apex Learning www.apexlearning.com/Solutions/online_courses.htm

There are also many virtual learning providers from state or city school districts, such as Kentucky Virtual High School, www.kvhs.org

Type of Equipment and Software

The type of computer equipment and software installed at your school will probably be determined by whoever makes the budget decisions in your school. If you have experience with hardware and software, you may be able to influence the purchase decision; if not let, someone with experience make this decision. The brand of computer you purchase will probably be determined by price and preference. In some cases, companies donate computers to a school district. This can be cost effective but can be restrictive because you must use the equipment that was donated, which could be outdated or not what you want or need. Most school districts are short on funding and therefore price should be considered but it should not be the only factor. Reliability and disk space are extremely important when deciding on the purchase of a computer. You will want a machine that has a large amount of disk space to store software and perhaps student's work. You should also be sure that the system contains the correct software such as the following:

- A composition tool such as Word, or WordPerfect
- A spreadsheet program such as Excel or Lotus 123
- A presentation program such as PowerPoint or Corel Presentations.

Although I used the Microsoft suite of products in my class that does not mean that they are the only software that should or could be used. Many other software products are available for both the PC and the Apple machines. In my school, as in many schools, the decision to use Microsoft software was made by the principal. The software and hardware was installed before I came to the school. Sometimes the decision will be made by the district and sometimes the decision will be made because the equipment is donated. Although most software products are similar, there are some differences between the Microsoft products and other software products.

The software listed below are for PC's. I did not list the very good software available for the Apple machines because Apple equipment was not used in my school and I am not as familiar with the Apple system.

Word Processing Software

Microsoft Word and Corel WordPerfect are the two major word processing products available today. PageMaker by Adobe is a desktop publishing system that is more practical to use when creating professional publications. Although I am familiar with all three products, PageMaker is far too sophisticated to use in school. WordPerfect is similar to Word and has many of the same menu icons (save, print, etc.). Because the products are so similar, either product can be used in class.

Spreadsheet Software

The three major spreadsheet products are Excel, Lotus 123 and Corel Quattro Pro. There are differences in the three products, especially in how calculations are performed (formulas) and in how charts are created. I have found that each product is better than the others in some way, making any selection acceptable. Normally, if you use Microsoft Office, WordPerfect Office, or Lotus SmartSuite you will have the full range of products from the software company.

Presentation Software

PowerPoint, Corel Presentations and Lotus Freelance Graphics are three popular software systems that can be used to create presentations. You may feel that this is not an important topic for students but I believe students should learn how to stand up and make a presentation using slides. It will give them more confidence and give them a better sense of worth. This topic can be taught from fourth grade to eight grades. I did teach this topic in most of my classes and in general the students enjoyed the experience.

In general all the products are the same; however each product has some strength. For example, I feel that Freelance Graphics software produces the most professional charts. Corel Presentations has more and different types of templates that can be used to create many different types of slides. All the products are reasonably easy to use.

Mail Software

There are many mail products on the market. Several that are available to you include Microsoft Outlook, Novell GroupWise, or Lotus Notes. You can also use mail software that comes with AOL or MSN or EarthLink. All of these products are different and contain different filtering devices. In your school, you will probably use the software that comes with your browser or Internet provider or you will use Outlook. The use of mail in your school can help students in many ways not the least of which include; assignment scheduling, help for students after hours, school activity calendar and more.

Internet Browsers

The two main Internet browsers are Microsoft Explorer and Netscape. They are not the same type of software as AOL or EarthLink or MSN; those products are Internet *providers* not browsers. There are differences in the browser software and how they treat some web code but generally either browser can be used without encountering many problems.

Web Creation Software

There are many software products available to produce web sites. Just some of these products include Microsoft FrontPage, DreamWeaver, Java, JavaScript, HTML as well as Microsoft Word. If you want to teach web design in your class, you should use a simple tool that will not cause confusion in the class. A later section of this book describes how to create a class web site.

Students today are interested in downloading music and pictures and therefore you will need the ability to store music and digital pictures based on the legal requirements in effect at the time.

In order to help the students and to safe guard their work I strongly recommend that each student have their own diskette or RW CD to store their assignments. This diskette will be purchased by the school, checked for virus, and then used by the student for the school year. At the beginning of each period, the student will be given their diskette, which will then be used in class. At the end of the period, the diskette will be given back to the teacher for protection.

I also recommend that if you have Internet access you install some firewall protection as protection from unwanted outside access. This could help protect your school's investment from malicious hacker attacks. In addition, I recommend a virus protection system such as Norton® or MacAfee® software. This will protect your system from inside attacks from bad diskettes or CD's. The virus protection software that you use will have to be updated periodically to ensure that you have the latest virus protection software. Because hackers constantly try new techniques, your machines need the latest virus software protection. You should always be sure that students do not bring in their own CD's or diskettes and that the school use only legally purchased and shrink-wrapped software.

Educational Software

When I first started teaching, I noticed a large amount of educational CD's left behind by the previous instructor. One of the first tasks I undertook was to evaluate which, if any of this software, could be useful in class. I discovered that software that I found interesting the students found boring. I also found that software that I found hard to understand, the students could learn quickly. I also found that there were not enough copies of the good software, which could be installed on all machines. This became a very difficult problem to solve.

One solution that I tried was to install different software on each machine. For example, if I had four copies of one title I would install the software on four machines then if I had six copies of a different title I would install that software on the next six machines. In this way, I would keep the software legal and try out different titles to see which ones the students liked and which ones were effective tools for learning. This solution did not work well. The company that supported the equipment wanted all machines to have the exact software on all machines. In the event of a problem, all they had to do was swap out the system disk that was pre-installed with all the software. This would allow easy replacement in the event of trouble. I could understand their point but it just was not working. There just was not enough software to go around and no money to buy more. Even though I was tempted to continue to install the software as described, I had to conform to the restrictions presented to me by the vendor and the school. This meant that there was never enough software for the students.

When writing this book I debated whether I should recommend educational software. I was never sure if I should recommend the software that I used however; the reason that you are reading this book is to gain information, so the following are my recommendations for software that both my students and I enjoyed. In some cases, the software was strictly educational, in others it helped in my reward system.

For educational software, I can recommend all of the Jumpstart software from Preschool to 4th grade. The pre-K through 3rd grade students really enjoyed this software and it was educational for them as well. For grades higher than fourth, the students in general did not want to use Jumpstart software. They liked using SIMM software, such as SIMM Town and SIMM Safari, and Pinball and *Who Wants to be a Millionaire®* as well as *Carmen Sandiego's Think Quick Challenge*. Of course, I would not let them use this software until all their assignments were completed. This led to another problem; students would rush through their assignments so they could play games. I would start every class assignment by telling the class not to rush through the assignment but in general, most students preferred to get a lower grade in order to have more time playing games.

Some software at first appeared to be child friendly but I soon found that the software was too hard or confusing to the students. One product, which shall remain nameless, proved to be so buggy that a student started to cry when she tried to use it. Clearly, I never used that software again.

Other software that the children enjoyed to use included: *Tonka Construction, Tonka Search and Rescue, The Land Before Time Movie Book* for ages 3-6, and *The*

Land Before Time Activity Center for ages 4-8. All of these products could be used in the early grades from pre-k through 4th grade.

There is additional education software available from many venders. Any teaching conference will include a presentation from various venders with the educational software that they sell. Much of the software is good or even very good, but it can also be expensive. At the end of this book, I list many of these venders and their web sites.

There are many products on the market that can be used to help teach students how to type. Just a few are:

- Type to Learn 3, Sunburst www.sunburst.com, grades 3 and up
- Typing Instructor for Kids, Individual Software, www.individualsoftware.com, grades 2-7
- Mavis Beacon Teaches Typing, Riverdeep, www.riverdeep.com, grades 3 and up
- Read, Write, and Type Learning System, Talking Fingers, www.readwritetype.com, grades 1-3.

MY SCHOOL'S SOFTWARE

Because my school used IBM PC's they used Microsoft Office products. There are good and bad reasons for this arrangement. The IBM type PC and Microsoft Office are the most popular products both in business and education; therefore, the students were learning to use the system and software that most people use. There are however; other systems on the market, in particular the Apple. The Apple system and software are both excellent and the hardware is less prone to hackers than the PC. There are very good educational software available for the Apple and there is no reason why this system and software could not be considered for your school.

The software listed below was used in my school and district.

Microsoft Word

Microsoft Word ® and to a lesser extent Notepad were the products that I used to teach typing and to introduce the students to word processing. Notepad was useful because there was no help assistant to fool with. The students, especially the young students, loved to use the help assistant instead of typing the assignment. When using Word the students would spend time setting up the assistant the way they wanted the assistant to appear (dog, cat, etc). Since each class was forty-five minutes long, I could not afford to wait for the students to play with the machines. Students also used a lot of time setting up special fonts and formats with which to type. Many assignments however required Word. In order to learn the advanced techniques of professional writing they had to become proficient with Word or some other similar product. There are many other good systems that could be used to learn how to type such as; WordPerfect, FrameMaker, Adobe and others but Word was the product that was installed on these machines and was what I used to teach typing. Besides using Word for typing assignments, I also did my best to teach the students some of the advanced techniques of Word, such as formatting, tabs, inserts and saving files. The senior classes did not need any instruction in these areas but they still needed to type faster. All the classes needed to be able to write better.

I noticed this issue regarding poor writing ability at the college level as well as in the early grades. Several of my students in college produced such poor reports that I had to request they take a writing course.

Microsoft Excel

Excel proved to be quite a challenge to teach because it is not easy to learn. When a topic is difficult to learn students tend to block out the teacher. What I tried to do was use some real life examples that the students might need to use Excel to solve. Several of these samples are included in a later section. I started to teach Excel at the fourth grade level. The students in this grade were not as good as the seventh or eight graders but they performed well on the assignments. Generally, I had to re-teach Excel for every assignment. The students just forgot how to use drop down formulas, etc from one class to another. Since the Excel projects were becoming progressively more difficult this forced me to extent some assignment over two periods. The first period would be a simple review and the students could start the assignment then save it. The second week they could finish the assignment in class. Later, you will find a sample of the Excel assignments that I used in class. In general, this subject should be taught to all students from sixth grade on. You can also introduce the concepts in the 4th and fifth grade.

Microsoft PowerPoint

Although PowerPoint® in general is not used as much in school as Word and Excel; however, I find it very useful. Most of my class presentations are written in PowerPoint and when I was in business, I often created presentations using PowerPoint. I wanted to teach this topic to the seventh and eight grades but I wound up teaching PowerPoint to all grades from fourth to eighth. At first I did have reservations about teaching PowerPoint to the lower grades, but they were very fast learners. The students had a lot of fun inserting clip art and sounds in their presentations. They also had a lot of fun creating unusual backgrounds for their presentations. PowerPoint can be used by the students in class to make presentations. It can be an effective tool for class presentations.

Microsoft Access

Microsoft Access ® is one of the Microsoft Office suite of products. This product allows users to create, update, query and print a database. As with many Microsoft products, Access comes with a Wizard to help in the design of a database. I gave a lot of thought into teaching this product but in the end, I decided that an introduction into the fundamentals of general database technology and Access would be useful for the seventh and eight grades. I did not assign any Access projects because I felt that this topic was far too difficult to teach at this level.

Microsoft Publisher

Microsoft Publisher ® is a very powerful product that I never used until I started to teach. Publisher only comes with Microsoft Office Professional ®. After I experimented with Publisher, I discovered how powerful the product was and I assigned many projects to the class. The assignments that I developed were used in classes fourth through eighth. Later in the book, I have listed several Publisher assignments. One assignment that I wanted to assign was the creation of a web site. I was not sure whether we should use Publisher or Word for this assignment but in the end, I finally decided that we would try to create a class web site but that we would use Word instead. Because of time constraints, the students were unable to complete the web assignment during my first year at the school. This very large project took too much class time. I later decided to create a computer club and have the club work on this project. I have included assignment specifications that can be used for this project in this book.

Those in the seventh and eighth grade had the most fun with this product. Even when the assignments were completed, they continued to experiment and create signs for their room or special posters. This was fine with me because it increased their knowledge and gave them more experience with using computers, which was the point of the class.

Microsoft Paint

The students loved to use Paint in class. When they finished their class assignment, they would sometimes use Paint to create a background screen for their computer. Some of the designs were very good and I encouraged them to use Paint. I felt that using their spare time in this way was better than letting them play a game in class. Many of the senior students, especially in the eighth grade, were very good with Paint. They could create sophisticated pictures that they then used as screen savers or backgrounds. The lower grades had much more difficulty using Paint. It seems that some form of artistic ability is necessary to use this product otherwise; your drawings will appear primitive. I did assign several easy assignments for the lower grades, both to give them something to do in class and to give them more experience using the mouse and the computer. In general, all students can learn to use this product but not all students can become proficient at it.

TEACHING SUCCESS AND FAILURES

This next section describes the problems that I had with each grade and when possible any success. The problems that I encountered and the attempts at resolution that I made were very different depending on the class.

Pre-K and Kindergarten

When I first started teaching pre-k and kindergarten, I thought that these classes would be the hardest classes to teach, but they became my favorite classes. The children liked being in class and they had fun with the learning CD's that were provided for them. I also enjoyed being around them and this made for a very good experience for all of us.

In general, children in these grades have poor computer and less developed motor skills. This does not mean however that they can't have a meaningful experience in a computer class. What I attempted to do when teaching these grades was to develop some motor skills by the use of educational software. The software I used helped the children learn to use the mouse and to use the computer to paint and draw and learn the alphabet and basic number series.

One issue that arose in these classes and to some extent the first and second grade was how noisy the students were. In pre-k and kindergarten, the students did not just talk and laugh, they would shriek. This was their way of laughing and it was very loud. I had a particular bad day with noise management once and the shrieking was especially loud because a large bug was in the class. The bug was of the water bug variety and it made the class very noisy because all the students wanted to see the bug and they all made noise about it. I made the situation worse when I tried to get rid of the bug but I had nothing with which to pick it up. As a solution, I stepped on the bug. This really got the class going. It took the rest of the period to quiet them down and I did learn a lesson, leave bugs alone!

To change the subject, in teaching the lower grades I relied mainly on education software to teach the students how to use the computer, the keyboard and the mouse. Most students, but not all, were quick learners. One or two students were intimidated by the computer and were even afraid to touch the mouse. Eventually, with a lot of patience, these students did gain enough confidence to use the machines. Another problem that occurred in these classes was sharing. Because the same software was not installed on every machine, some students would have to use one product while others would use another product. This caused problems because not everyone wanted to share what they were using. Some software became more popular than other software and everyone wanted to use it. This meant that I had to distribute the software and students as best as I could and try to maintain control of any differences the students might have.

Students in these grades also became much more frustrated when they experienced problems than the other grades. If the software did not work, or if I could not get to them fast enough they would some times cry. Sharing software became a big issue because some software was much more popular than other software. The boys also wanted to use different software than the girls therefore I had to distribute the software very carefully.

First Grade and Second Grade

These grades were interesting because the students were just starting to learn and they had developed some motor skills, which would allow them to learn more "complex" computer skills. Since the children were learning to read and write, I used many typing assignments in class. I soon discovered how important that was when I saw how poorly the older students typed. Even students in the seventh and eighth grade had a hard time typing with any speed and accuracy. Since my principal wanted me to spend a lot of time teaching the students typing, that is what I did for these early grades. Sometimes I would bring in an article that I found and sometimes I would bring in a copy of a few paragraphs from a story such as The *Cat In The Hat* ©. I also managed to write a few of my own stories for the class to type. I have included several of my typing assignments in this book.

The second grade also presented me with some of my more difficult problems. This was my largest class and not every one in class could use their own computer. This required several students to use one computer. Because I graded these students, those students that shared a machine would have to share the grade, that is, each would get the same grade. This was not always fair to the students in several regards. First, usually with two students at a machine, one student would type and one would watch. I tried to have the students' share the work but they often did not share. If a good typist was doing the work both students would get a good mark, however if the poor student was typing then the good typist would get a poorer grade then they deserved. I also had several excellent students in this class, students who were so far beyond the typing skills of the other students that it was a waste of time to have them type. To help those students and make better use of their time I gave them pre-Excel software to use in class. This caused an additional issue; the other students wanted to know why "John" and "Mary" were playing games while they had to type! The second grade gave me a lot of experience in teaching and class management.

Third Grade

The third grade students were about eight years old and offered me a different challenge. I could not use simple typing exercises as I did with the first and second grade yet I knew that they needed to improve their typing and writing skills. I did have an educational CD that taught typing and that the students enjoyed, but I only had three copies of this CD and I was unable to purchase any more. This left me with few alternatives but to find interesting articles and then have the students' type them in class. The students very quickly became bored of the typing assignments. One method that I used to try to overcome this difficulty was by rewarding the students. I actually used this technique in all the grades from second through eight. I would give the students an exercise to perform in class and when they completed the exercise, I would allow them to play with one of the games on CD. This worked out better than I expected. Once the other students saw some one playing a game they would quickly become motivated to finish the assignment. This was also a problem because students tried to complete the assignment quickly so that they could play games. This usually meant that they did a poor job on the assignment and therefore could receive a poor grade. To prevent the students from receiving a poor grade I would review their completed assignments before allowing them to play a game. If the assignment was acceptable they could use a game if not they would have to go back and complete the assignment correctly.

I did experiment with Microsoft Publisher with this grade but in general, the students could not perform the assignments as well as the other older students. I also experimented with Microsoft Paint. The students did enjoy this product almost as much as a game and I allowed the students to use it when they correctly finished their typing assignment.

Fourth Through Sixth Grade

The 4th through 6th grades required the most work and involvement. I had to prepare new assignments constantly in order to help the students learn. One of the major tasks that I asked the students to perform was to do a lot of typing. I also introduced Excel and PowerPoint to this and all older students. Some students took well to the assignments but others did not. I had one particular student, a boy, who refused to do any work. When it came time to grade him I was torn between giving him a zero, which would cause all sorts of questions by his teacher and the principal, or to just not give him a grade or to give him an incomplete as a grade. In the end, I decided to give him a grade of incomplete. This would imply that he did not do the exercise but would not generate any questions. In effect, the grade did generate many questions. Fortunately, this student performed the same in all his classes; therefore it was easy to defend his grade. I received many phone calls and had to defend myself to many other parents of students who received an incomplete.

Typing in these grades, as in most grades, was an important task that the principal and I wanted the students to perform. This was necessary because most students had very poor typing, composition and spelling skills. Most of the students could barely type a short paragraph in the forty-five minute class. Besides typing, the student's composition skills were exceptionally poor. They could not spell or compose a simple report. As I discovered this deficiency, I added more and more report writing and typing to the class curriculum.

Personally, I believe that the two most important skills that a student should learn are reading and writing. Writing may not seem to be a necessary part of a computer class, but by integrating typing with writing, I felt that I was doing the students a favor. They were learning two skills that they would surely need later in high school.

Seventh and Eight Grade

In my school, the seventh grade was better behaved than the eight grade but not by much. As the year progressed, the situation changed and the seventh grade became quite noisy and the eighth grade became a little quieter. This may have been a result of all the tests the eighth grade was taking. The eighth grade took a series of tests for high school admissions as well as the required assessment tests. From what I could see, both the girls and the boys in the seventh and eighth grade were noisy, did not want to do any work, and in general were disruptive.

This may have had something to do with their knowledge that they were seniors or almost seniors and that they would be leaving at the end of the year. They may have felt that they could do what they wanted to do. It took quite some time before this idea changed. One way I tried to overcome this problem was with grading. This came as a big shock to the students. My grades were to be included with the other teacher's grades for an overall grade. This later changed and my grade became an official grade on their report card. This could be an issue for those students who were applying for a good high school. In general, most of the students performed the exercises assigned to them but they still made too much noise. I was constantly playing a game of musical chairs to separate those students who were making noise. The speakers became one of the big noisemakers in this class. The students continued to use the speakers and headsets even when they were told that they could not. Finally, I had to disconnect the speakers before every eight-grade class. This added to my workload, but gave me more noise control. The eighth grade students also started to bring in music CD's and this became a large issue. No one was allowed to bring in personal CD's or diskettes. I had to confiscate the CD's and I also printed a list of rules (see below) that I posted on each machine. This set of rules included the following:

Computer Class Rules
• No personal CD's or diskettes allowed in class
• No food or drinks allowed in class
• No talking in class
• No disruptive behavior
• No game CD's unless directed by the teacher
• No leaving your desk or the room.
• No powering down of system
• No modifying system
Detention IS an option.

Except for the food and drink rule, the students did not pay much attention to the other rules. The last rule was very important because the students loved to change the screen layout. They would make their own screen saver or background using Paint. At the end of the day, I then had to reset the machines back to the system defaults.

LESSONS, CLASS ASSIGNMENTS, AND EXAMS

In order to be able to differentiate the students and grade them fairly, it is necessary to give the students exams. In addition it was necessary to give them lessons during class. It was not sufficient to let the students work on the computers without any direction because they will cause chaos and they can damage the machines. What follows are my suggestions for lessons and a large number of class assignments.

Lessons

When I first started teaching, I had just a vague idea of what to do. I knew that I wanted to teach the normal useful subjects such as Microsoft Word, and PowerPoint, but I did not know if Excel would be a good idea. I also wanted to see if the 7th and 8th grade could design and code a class web site in competition with the other class. However, beyond that I did not have a clue. I soon discovered that it was worse than that. The classes wanted to do anything but work; they wanted to play games. This attitude was a left over from the previous instructor. The previous instructor let the class play games in class and did very little if any teaching. My idea was to teach and then reward those who completed assignments by allowing them to play games. At first, this did not work because the students did not want to use the time for anything other than games. The way I tried to resolve this issue was by grading the students. As previously noted, the class was not scheduled to be graded. This made class management difficult. The students treated the class as recess. I initially tried to give set seat assignments to break up the cliques, but this did not work because the students still tended to work their way back to wherever they wanted to sit. Then I decided to grade the students and give these grades to their class teacher. My grade would be included in the students overall grade. This got the students attention and made life easier. For me. The students did not like being graded, even though I was an easy grader. Eventually my grade would become an official grade on their report card. This also became an issue. After the students received their first report card, some became upset with their grade. Their parents became even more upset. I spent the better part of a week on the phone with parents explaining how I developed their child's grade. In some cases, I had to send a written report home every week explaining how a child had performed that week. The workload of teaching every student in the school (300) was becoming unbearable.

Assessment Exams

In my school, as in others in New York State, students are required to take assessment exams. These exams are designed to see what the students know on particular topics such as math and social studies. They are not only used to grade the students but also the school. How the students perform is a reflection on how well the teachers taught the topics. Many teachers believe that this is teaching to the test. I agree with that statement. You must teach the students what will be on the test and how to take the test and not what you may want to teach.

In order to help the students and the school I tried to develop some assessment tests related to computers and math and integrate them in my class. I would have the students type the answers to the exam in order for them to get even more experience in typing.

Later in this book, I have included several exams that I developed and gave to the 7th and 8th grade to take. I also had the 6th grade type the exam in class. This gave them a feel for the exams and gave them experience in typing. The students really did not enjoy taking these tests and soon became rebellious. Their rebellion took the form of not doing the exam. This caused me to question if I had explained the importance of the tests enough or did the students just get tired of taking tests in all their classes. In the end, I stopped giving the exams.

Class Assignments

The following are the class assignments that I used listed by grade. In many cases, the same assignment was used for many classes. In these situations, I have identified how the assignments were used. It was important for me to be creative with my assignments in order to get the students attention and to give them experience and something to do. Not all assignments kept the students attention because students wanted to have too much fun in class and assignments, no matter how creative I was with them, just were not fun.

One early assignment I gave to all the classes was to be used to help develop the students typing skills. This was something that the principal wanted to see improved. The assignment that I gave to the 4th through 8th grade was to type what they wanted to learn in class that year. Part two of the assignment was to write what place they went to where they had the best time. I left them to define what best meant to them. This assignment was used not only to reinforce their typing skills but also to make them think. The responses gave me a look into their lives and told me a lot about the students. I expected the normal answers like a beach or Disney World or some similar spot. Several of the responses made me think that the students had more problems at home than anything I could hope to solve in my class.

Pre-K and Kindergarten

For these grades, I used the educational software and for kindergarten, I tried to integrate some basic typing into the class. In general, I used examples from famous books, such as *The Cat in the Hat* for the students. The students may not have understood all the words but at least they could get the feel for the keyboard. I did not attempt any typing for pre-k. For the pre-k class I only used software that allowed the students to paint, learn the letters and in general become familiar with the computer. I also tried to teach them how to respect the computer and what to do and not do (power off!) when using the computer.

Students in these grades were fun to be around and fun to teach. Everything was a new experience for them. For Pre-k, their teacher accompanied them to the class and was in attendance for the period. This was the only grade for which this was true. For all other grades included kindergarten I was left alone to teach the students. This was different from prior years when a senior would assist for each class. This was an experiment that the new principal was trying. I don't believe the experiment was a success because it led to confusion and noise problems.

First and Second Grades

Although these students were very young, (6-7) the students had the motor coordination to attempt typing assignments. The second grade, for whatever reason, was one of my nosiest classes. The boys were always annoying the girls and several times, I had to send the disruptive boys to the principal's office. Noise was one thing but being disruptive in class was not acceptable to me. When the students went to the principal's office they had to stay there for the period and they lost some school privileges. Being sent to the principal's office was not taken lightly in this school.

The following are some of the short stories that I wrote, and that were used in my first, second and third grade class as a typing assignment. The stories are not Hemingway but I felt that the stories were good for those ages and grades to read and type. The stories had a theme and a lesson to learn and the students could also learn to do some reading. No one typed very much of the story, but most students did at least try to read the story. In most cases the stories were too difficult for the students to read therefore I read the story before they attempted to type the story.

Assignment 1

The Little Red Ball and the Big Fir Tree
Salvatore Mamone

Not too long ago, on a pleasant farm, lived a little boy name Jeff. Jeff was 6 years old and he lived with his mother and father on a large farm in the middle of farm country. Now Jeff, like most little boys, had many toys to play with; but his favorite was a little red ball. He would kick the ball and throw the ball and run after the ball and sometimes he even went to sleep with the ball. The little red ball was his favorite toy, which made the little red ball very happy. But one-day dad brought home a toy soldier for Jeff's birthday. When Jeff saw the toy soldier he laughed and smiled, just the way he did with the little red ball. But now with the toy soldier Jeff had no time for the little red ball. Sometimes Jeff even forgot his chores, like milking the cows. Jeff's mom and dad did not know what to do. "If only Jeff would play with his little red ball like before," his father said. "At least before he made time for other things, like school work and house chores. Oh woe what to do?" said Jeff's father.

Now it happened that one windy day the little red ball rolled out the open kitchen door and struck a big fir tree. This fir tree was the biggest Christmas tree that any one had ever seen. It was much too big to be cut down and used in the house at Christmas. When the little red ball struck the big fir tree, the fir tree said,
"Who is that"?
"It is just I, a little red ball".
"Well then why did you hit me"?
"The wind blew me out the door and into you. Sorry".
"Hum," said the big fir tree, "A likely story".
"But it's true. My owner just left me on the floor and I blew out the door".
"Well why doesn't he play with you"?
"Because he has a new toy to play with".

"Hum" said the big fir tree, "Can't you tell him how you feel"?

"But my owner doesn't speak ball", cried the little red ball.

"Yes I guess humans are not smart enough to speak ball. Well maybe we should try something else".

"Like what?" said the little red ball.

"I don't know let me think. Hmm. Hmm."

"Wait a minute", said the little red ball, "I may have an idea".

"Well don't keep me shaking my leaves, what is it?"

"What if the new toy were to disappear somehow?"

"What do you mean?"

"Well I can do something the toy soldier can't do, I can roll!"

"And what good is that?"

"Well if I can roll the toy soldier to someplace that Jeff would never look, maybe he would forget about the new toy and play with me again."

"You know that is just ball enough to work," said the big fir tree.

And so the little red ball rolled back into the house and into the bedroom where the toy soldier stood guard over the bed.

"Well look who is back." said the toy soldier, "What brings you here into *my* room."

"It is not your room, it was and still is my room." said the little red ball.

"Yes of course it is, is that why you need to go outside just to have someone to talk to? Ha."

"We will see who has the last laugh my military friend."

And with that, the little red ball rolled and rolled and rolled and the toy soldier did not look so brave anymore. And now with one final roll the little red ball pushed the toy soldier to a place that Jeff would never look, under the bureau. When the toy soldier was completely under the bureau, the little red ball felt happy and sad. He was happy to be rid of the toy soldier, but sad because he was sure that what he had done was not a nice thing to do. Well the little red ball said; let us see what Jeff thinks when he gets home. When Jeff came home from school, he went and looked for his favorite new toy, the toy soldier. Now Jeff looked and looked and looked but the toy soldier was nowhere to be found. "Oh no" said Jeff, "where is my toy soldier? What could have happen to him?" And then Jeff did something that made the little red ball sad. Jeff started to cry. The little red ball had never seen the boy cry before and the little red ball did not know what to do. "I think I may have done a bad thing," he said, "But how can I fix it".

That night the little red ball thought long and hard about what he had done and how he could fix it. He wanted to be popular but was it worth it to make a little boy cry. The little red ball no longer thought so. And with that thought he rolled over to the bureau and pushed the toy soldier out where Jeff could see him when Jeff woke up in the morning.

The next morning Jeff was still sad about the toy soldier and tired because he did not sleep well. But then he saw the toy soldier and next to it the little red ball. "Oh yes", said Jeff, "I found my toy soldier. Where have you been?" "And look my little red ball too. I haven't seen you in a while either. What a great day this is." And Jeff smiled and started to play with the toy soldier and the little red ball, until all three of them were too tired to play any more. "This has been such a happy day" said Jeff. And the little red ball agreed.

Later after every one was too tired to play and with the window open and the wind blowing, the little red ball rolled to the open window and was pointing, or looking, at the big fir tree. Now with the wind blowing Jeff could hear all sorts of noise, some of which sounded like talking; but little red balls and big fir trees can't talk, can they?

Assignment 2—The Adventures of Fudge and Samantha

The next typing assignment, which I gave to the first through third grade, was about two of my cats, Fudge and Samantha. I thought that a story about animals might get the students attention. I read the story to the class and than I asked the students try to type the story. In most cases, the students could barely type one or two sentences.

The Adventures of Fudge and Samantha
Salvatore Mamone

Fudge the cat did not appear at my doorstep, nor was she bought at some pet store; she was adopted at a pound like her best cat friend Samantha. Fudge was a very pretty calico cat and Samantha was a beautiful tuxedo cat. A calico cat is usually female and has many colors like brown and black and orange and white. A tuxedo cat is black and white and looks like she is wearing a tuxedo. Look at the picture below to see how beautiful they were.

When they were both kittens they would run around the house like it was the best thing to do and to them it was. One trick they liked to play was to scratch their paws on the wallpaper. This made them very happy but did not make the wallpaper look good. Another thing that Fudge liked to scratch was the Christmas tree. The Christmas tree made a perfect scratch post for her. Samantha of course was too much of a lady to do such a thing. Samantha would cross her paws and look at Fudge and in some cat way you just know that she was thinking "Isn't that just like a bad kitten".

Samantha was always a lady but she was still the boss cat in the house. She would sit on the highest place she could find and everyone else would have to look up to her as if she was the queen. Fudge just liked to eat and sleep. She could always tell when it was time to eat. Whenever we used the can opener, she just knew that the food was for her even if it was people food. She would then come running and push Samantha out of the way and eat first. That is probably why Fudge was so big and Samantha was so thin and lady-like.

Assignment 3—The Christmas Wish

This next story was written for a Christmas assignment. The assignment was given to the first through third grade to type. I felt that it had a nice message and was fairly easy to type. The story was written in all capitals because my wife suggested that it might be easier for the students to read and to type.

THE CHRISTMAS WISH
Salvatore Mamone

PETER, UNLIKE MOST CHILDREN, WAS NOT WAITING FOR CHRISTMAS TO HURRY UP AND GET HERE. HE KNEW THAT HE WOULD RECEIVE ALL KINDS OF NICE TOYS AND CLOTHES. BUT WHAT HE WANTED MOST OF ALL FOR CHRISTMAS WAS TO SEE HIS GRANDFATHER AGAIN. HIS GRANDFATHER WAS A VERY BIG AND TALL MAN WITH BIG FEET AND EVEN BIGGER HANDS. IF YOU WERE TO SEE HIM IN PERSON YOU MIGHT BE AFRAID OF HIM, BUT PETER KNEW THAT HIS GRANDFATHER WAS A VERY GENTLE MAN. HIS GRANDFATHER LIKED TO HELP PETER WITH HIS HOMEWORK. HE ALSO LIKED TO HELP PETER PAINT PICTURES. PETER AND HIS GRANDFATHER WOULD SPEND HOURS OUTSIDE PAINTING THE SKY AND THE TRESS AND THE BIRDS.

THIS YEAR CHRISTMAS WOULD NOT BE AS MUCH FUN FOR PETER BECAUSE HE KNEW THAT HIS GRANDFATHER WOULD NOT BE HERE. PETER'S GRANDFATHER DIED JUST BEFORE THANSK-GIVING. LOTS OF PEOPLE CAME TO THE HOUSE TO SAY HOW SORROW THEY WERE BUT NO ONE WAS SORRIER THAN PETER. THE TIME BETWEEN THANKSGIVING AND CHRISTMAS WENT FAST BUT NOT FAST ENOUGH FOR PETER TO FORGET. MORE THAN ANYTHING HE WISHED THAT HE COULD SEE HIS GRANDFATHER FOR CHRISTMAS.

WHEN CHRISTMAS DAY ARRIVED PETER OPENED HIS GIFTS, HAD BREAKFAST, AND GOT DRESSED FOR CHURCH. EVEN WITH ALL THE GIFTS HE WAS NOT FELLING HAPPY. HE DID NOT GET WHAT HE WANTED MOST, TO SEE HIS GRANDFATHER AGAIN. HIS DAD TOLD HIM THAT IT WAS IMPOSSIBLE BUT PETER JUST KNEW THAT HIS GRANDFATHER WOULD FIND A WAY.

WHEN IT WAS TIME TO GO TO CHURCH PETER AND HIS FAMILY GOT THEIR COATS AND STARTED TO LEAVE THE HOUSE WHEN ALL OF A SUDDEN THE BIGGEST AND BRIGHTEST RAINBOW THAT ANYONE HAD EVER SEEN APPEARED. EVERYONE SAID HOW STRANGE THAT WAS; RAINBOWS DON'T APPEAR JUST LIKE THAT ESPECIALLY THIS LATE IN THE YEAR. HOWEVER, PETER KNEW

BETTER. HE KNEW THAT GRANDFATHER HAD COME BACK FOR CHRISTMAS.

Assignment 4—The Big Game

This typing assignment was given to the first through fourth grade. It is not one of my better stories but it was not used as a reading assignment but rather was used to help the students improve on their poor typing ability. I asked the students to use special fonts and font sizes for this assignment.

The Big Game
Salvatore Mamone

Basketball was a very big sport at my school; so big that some people would rather play basketball than do school work. The school usually had a good team because so many boys wanted to play. The girls wanted to play too but the school did not have enough female students to field a basketball team. This year the team was very good, good enough to challenge for the city championship. The only thing standing in the way of the championship was the last game of the season and the team captain's bad leg.

The team captain had hurt his leg the week before in a hard played game against one of the poorer teams in the league. The other team was not expected to be much of a challenge but that is why they were. They had nothing to lose and we took them lightly. That was an important lesson for the team and the school. Now with the championship on the line our team captain was hurting and last year's championship team was the opponent. The coach tried to motivate the team as best as he could but everyone was very concerned. This was the closest the school had ever come to playing for the city championship and no one knew when they would get another chance.

The day of the game the school held a rally in the cafeteria to try to get the rest of the school behind the team. The school also held a rally after school in the parking lot. Everyone made a lot of noise and everyone had a lot of fun but everyone was still unsure how the team would play without its captain.

On the day of the big game there were no empty seats in the gym and many people were standing in the aisle. The captain of the team was limping and his replacement was very nervous. This was the game of the year and as far as everyone knew the game of their life.

The game started fast with the other team scoring the first 8 points. Then it was our turn to start playing. For the rest of the first period we managed to stay close but we could not overtake the other team. By the half we were down by 11 points and everyone started to doubt that we could come back. During the second half we managed to cut the lead to 8 points but we still could not break through. With the entire school screaming we were able to cut the lead to a final 4 points but it was not enough. Our championship would have to wait. In any game there has to be a winner and a loser, but in this game we may have lost but we played like winners.

This next assignment was given only to the first and second grades. My intent was to write a small story with short sentences in the hope this would help the students finish the assignment in class. Even with this short story the students could not finish the assignment in one class.

Walking My Dog

I am big enough to walk my dog.
My dog is a collie just like Lassie.
She is called Lassie.
In the morning, Lassie knows that I will take her for a walk.
I take her for a walk before breakfast.
My dad comes with me.
He lets me help with the leash.
At night, it is too dark for me to walk the dog.
My dad walks Lassie at night.
Some people think that walking the dog is work.
I think it is fun.

Third Grade

Creating assignments for the third grade was very difficult. I never felt that they were mature enough to learn Excel or even PowerPoint therefore; I concentrated on using typing to keep the class involved. Like many of the other grades the third grade soon became bored with the typing assignments and I became bored with having to develop typing assignments. Because I needed to respond to the principal's request to improve the students typing speed and accuracy, I needed to give typing assignments to the class. The following are several assignments that I gave to the third through the eight grades. The assignments were used to help the students' type faster and also to think.

Assignment 1—The Best Place You Ever Visited

Type, in as much detail as required, a report on the best place you ever visited. Include in this assignment, what your definition of best is.

This assignment caused some difficulty because the students thought I was talking about the best place they visited over the summer. Some students mistakenly thought I meant for them to describe what they did over the summer. I was very surprised with some of the answers from this assignment. In some cases, the students gave normal responses such as a beach, etc. But in some cases, the students gave me too much insight into their home life.

This next assignment was used for the third grade but could also be used for the fourth, fifth and sixth grades.

Assignment 2 Fantasy Invention

Type, in as much detail as required, a report on a fantasy invention. This could be something that you want to invent or that you wish someone else would invent. Be as specific as possible. Explain why you want to see this invention built.

This seemed like a straightforward lesson but the class could not get the hang of it. There were very few creative answers to this assignment. As with most writing assignments, there were many misspellings and grammar errors. Because of the typing errors, I used one period to work with the students on the use of the spell checker, but they did not get the hang of how to use this feature. I thought about changing the setup for Word to automatically correct text as the student typed but I decided against it. I wanted the students to see the mistakes they were making.

If you would like to setup your machine to automatically correct spelling errors, you just need to do the following.

- On the *Tools* menu, click *AutoCorrect Options*.
- Select the check boxes you wish to use, especially the *Replace text as you type* check box.

Assignment 3—Robot

I used this assignment in the third through sixth grade. I expected most students to pick being the robot and the majority of students did. The students who wanted to remain a human gave that answer because they did not want to give up compassion or feeling.

Type; in as much detail as possible your answer to the following.

Consider the following:

You are a robot who actually looks just like you. You do not have human qualities such as compassion, you cannot enjoy simple things such as music and eating, but you do have different qualities such as the following four: super strength, the ability to see great distances, the ability to never die (unless there is a severe mechanical failure) and the ability to think faster than a human. These are your *only* super powers.

Write a short piece that has a beginning, middle and end, that will describe how your life would be different as a robot and if you think it would it be better. Use bold font, type size of 12 and type of Times New Roman.

This very straightforward assignment caused a great deal of trouble. For some reason the class added powers to the robot, which I did not specify. They were again not very creative in their response and in general did not answer the question as required. With this assignment, I started to grade with more gusto. In order to get an A they truly had to do what was required.

I discussed this assignment later with another teacher and she told me that the problem with the assignment was that the assignment was too difficult. I should have just asked them to describe what it would be like to be a robot. I guess in a way the assignment might be too difficult for some students to understand, but I always felt that students are smarter than they appear.

Assignment 4—Your School

This assignment was only used in the third grade. I felt that it was too simple for grades four through eight but too hard for first and second grade. In general, the third grade had a lot of fun with this assignment.

> What if you had to explain your school to someone who could not understand words, like someone from another planet? This alien could however understand pictures. Using Word, and clip art, design and create a <u>picture only</u> document that can describe your school to the alien.

Assignment 5—NASA

In my search for interesting exercises for the class to perform, I discovered a contest run by NASA. The intent of the contest was to have schools compete with each other for the right to send an experiment in to space on the space shuttle. While searching the NASA web site for information on this contest I discovered the following exercise and I thought that it might be fun for the students to work on in class. The intent, as were many of my exercises, was to get the students to think. I gave the exercise to all grades from fourth through eight. The answers the students gave ranged all over the map. Some students could not understand what the assignment meant.

Mars Trip

This assignment comes from the NASA web site.

You and your crew are about to blast off to Mars! Now you must decide what to take on the long journey in space.

The spaceship that will take you on the 9-month journey to Mars is already in a "parking orbit" around Earth. Everything you will need after you get to Mars has already been sent ahead to the red planet.

The orbiting Mars spaceship already contains everything you need to stay alive: air, food, water, and heaters.

However, you need to decide what else to take. For example, what favorite foods and beverages will you want to take? In addition, how will you pass the time?

You will be allowed to take only 10 items. Just remember, some things that work fine on Earth will cause problems in zero gravity!

If you like music, you may want to take a CD player and some CD's, but the CD player is one item and each CD is also an item. The same holds true for a DVD player and DVD music or videos. You may not take any person or animal with you.

Please describe the 10 items and why you picked each item. Please put your name and grade on the paper. You may use <u>up to</u> 2 small clip art inserts if you wish. Please use a font of size 12, Ariel normal and borders of 1 ½ inches on the top and bottom and 1 ¼ on both sides.

Assignment 6 PC Calculator Exercise

In an attempt to give more computer experience to the third grade, I introduced an exercise using the built-in calculator. This seemed like a good idea but I soon discovered that this exercise was far too simple for the students. I modified the exercise and gave a more difficult exercise to the fourth grade (see later).

Using the built-in PC calculator complete the following exercise.

1. Add the following numbers.
    10
    3
    5
    6
    12   Answer _____

2. Subtract 134 from 241   Answer _____

3. Add the following numbers

    12
    13
    6
    7
    8   Answer _____

4. Subtract 123 from 345   Answer _____

5. Add the following numbers
    12
    13
    14   Answer _____

6. Add the following numbers
    245
    367   Answer _____

7. Subtract 123 from 345   Answer _____

8. Subtract 123 from 546   Answer _____

9. Add the following numbers
      345
      2
      45
      67   Answer _____

10. Subtract 123 from 345   Answer _____

Assignment 7—Paint—Holiday Season

This assignment was used in the third and fourth grade and involved Paint. Most of the students had fun with the assignment while others insisted on using Word so that they could use clip art. I had to discourage them from using Word so that they could learn at least the fundamentals of Paint.

> Using Paint, create a picture of what *any* holiday season, such as Christmas or the Fourth of July means to you. This can include any religious meaning or some other meaning such as the change in the season. I should be able to tell how you feel about the holiday just by looking at the picture, words will not be needed.

Assignment 8—Publisher—Class President

This assignment was given to all grades from fourth through eighth. The intent was to have them be as creative as possible but also give them more experience with Publisher. In general, the eighth grade really enjoyed using Publisher. They would use publisher to create signs for their room at home. I let them be as creative as they wanted since this was also a learning experience. This assignment was to last for two periods because the students were required to create two forms. The assignment was not difficult but some of the students did have difficulty completing the assignment in two weeks while other students completed the assignment in one class.

Microsoft Publisher Assignment—Class President

Please put your name and grade on the paper. Failure to do so will result in you not receiving a grade.

This is a __TWO__ period assignment so I expect a good job. Before you leave class today, you should save your documents as follows:

- At the top of the menu bar click *File* then *Save As*
- Select the diskette drive (D) and then type in the file name box your first, last name, and the number 1 or 2 depending on which of the two documents you are saving, as in JohnBrown1. Now click ok.
- Next week you will open these files to complete your assignment.

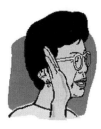

You have decided to run for class president. Because this is an elected position you need to have the other students in the school and class know who you are and what you stand for. Try to be as honest as you can.

Create a flyer that can be posted in your school *and* a handout that you can give to students. This flyer and handout are two separate documents. The flyer can use large fonts, bold type, etc to describe your candidacy for class president. The small handout can describe why you should be the class president.

HINTS

One way to create the flyer is by using the *Flyer -> Announcement* template. Change the text to fit your candidacy. Another way to create the flyer is with a *Sign* template.

One way to create the handouts is by using one of the announcement templates. Another way could be by using a business card template.

YOU decide what form to use.

Assignment 9—Time Capsule

I used this exercise in the third through the sixth grade. The intent once again was to reinforce the students writing and cognitive skills and to give them more experience with Word.

Time Capsule

You are currently a very young student in school. Based on estimates you will probably live at least another eighty-five years and reach the age of 100! Your assignment is the following: you are to "build" a time capsule that will be opened by you or your heirs when you would be 100 years old. The capsule will be a small footlocker that measures 3 feet long by 2 feet wide by 2 feet deep. The capsule will be placed somewhere it will be safe for eighty to ninety years.

Decide on the items you would place in the capsule. The items should be something that you would like to see again to remind yourself of when you were young. The items could be: a book, CD, movie, food, etc. NO living item. Pick at least 15 items to include and tell me why you picked the item.

Remember the size restriction of the footlocker. You may use a limited amount of clipart. You should use a font of size 12 and Times New Roman for this assignment.

Assignment 10—Space CD

The following was another assignment that I used to help improve students writing skills. It should be obvious by now that I am interested in space exploration.

The Space CD

As usual, this exercise was used to help the students think. The answers however were not very creative and in general, the students did a poor job with this assignment. This was a refection on the students rushing through the work and the student's poor writing skills.

Many years ago, the United States sent a satellite into space with a message on it just in case an intelligent civilization on another planet found it. This satellite contained pictures of a man and woman, instructions on Earth's location in the solar system and a greeting.

Your assignment is to create a CD of your own that will travel on a satellite to a far away universe. What writing and pictures would you put on this CD and why? Remember, aliens do not understand English. This assignment should be of font size 14, and font type Arial.

Assignment 11—Time Machine

A remake of the movie Time Machine had just hit movie theaters when I came up with this assignment. I do not know how many students were able to see the movie because of age restrictions but the assignment was still useful. This assignment was used for the third through sixth grade but it can probably be used for other grades as well.

The Time Machine

Suppose you found a time machine similar to the time machine in the movie *Back to the Future* or *The Time Machine*. You could go to any time in the past or future. Your assignment is to write a report, of at least three paragraphs, that will describe the following:

- When in time would you like to go and why?
- What do you expect to find when you arrive?
- Once there, would you want to come back? Why?

Please use a font size of 12 and use font type of Arial, use top and bottom margins of 1 ½ inches.

Assignment 12 Historical Person

This assignment was used in the third through sixth grades. I have often been intrigued by this question and I wondered what the students would think and write. Most students gave similar answers, similar to what you might expect, but no one gave the answer that I would have given; Americans have gone to the moon.

Please complete the following in class; you should use bold text and 12-point font. Please use margins of ¾ inches on all sides. Complete three paragraphs for this assignment.

Imagine Thomas Jefferson could some how come back from the dead! If he could see the world today, what would he find most amazing about how we have advanced as a country? What invention or event would most amaze him and why? Do you think he would like what has become of the world? Why?

Fourth Grade

In this grade, I started to introduce concepts of Excel and PowerPoint. Some teachers may feel that it is too early to teach these topics but I disagree. The class did very well on easy topics for both these products. I even went so far as to introduce charts in Excel to the class and they did very well understanding the concept. The following are several Excel assignments that I gave to the grades 4th through 8th. In general, all the students were able to understand the principles and received excellent grades for the assignments.

In assignment 1, I wanted to teach the fundaments of Excel and the formula box. For this assignment, I asked the class to type the data as shown but use the drop down box to create the averages and total averages.

Assignment 1—Excel—Class Average

Excel Assignment # 1							
Class		Grade 1	Grade 2	Grade 3	Grade 4	Grade 5	Average
Gym		95	83	92	83	84	87.4
Art		94	82	82	83	83	84.8
Music		81	74	82	81	82	80
Spanish		82	82	83	81	82	82
Computer		82	81	83	81	81	81.6
Math		92	91	92	83	92	90
Social Studies		81	82	82	82	73	80
History		91	81	82	92	82	85.6
English		81	90	91	92	82	87.2
Religion		93	94	93	94	84	91.6
Total Average							85.02

Assignment 2—Expenses

This special assignment was for those students who already knew Excel and could easily do the first assignment. I only gave this assignment to the seventh and eight grades. Only one student, in the seventh grade, was able to attempt this assignment and he could not complete it.

Date	Item	Price	Date	Item	Price	Date	Item	Price
7/1/2001	CD's	15.4	8/1/2001	movie	18	9/1/2001	food	8
7/1/2001	sweater	42	8/2/2001	clothes	59	9/1/2001	food	9
7/2/2001	movie	15	8/3/2001	food	7	9/2/2001	food	7
7/3/2001	food	20	8/3/2001	movie	12	9/3/2001	food	12
7/4/2001	food	12	8/4/2001	food	5	9/4/2001	movie	16
7/4/2001	food	14	8/5/2001	food	7	9/5/2001	food	10
7/5/2001	movie	18	8/6/2001	food	9	9/6/2001	food	10
7/10/2001	shoes	125	8/7/2001	food	7	9/7/2001	CD	13
7/11/2001	food	21	8/7/2001	food	14	9/8/2001	sneakers	125
7/12/2001	class trip	35	8/8/2001	CD's	16	9/9/2001	food	12
7/13/2001	CD's	17.3	8/10/2001	food	11	9/10/2001	food	11
7/15/2001	food	4.5	8/11/2001	food	11	9/11/2001	food	11
7/16/2001	food	8	8/12/2001	movie	19	9/11/2001	CD	10
7/17/2001	school sp	19	8/13/2001	CD's	15	9/12/2001	food	12
7/19/2001	food	11	8/14/2001	food	9	9/13/2001	movie	23
7/20/2001	movie	20	8/15/2001	food	9	9/14/2001	CD player	120
7/21/2001	CD's	13	8/16/2001	clothes	69	9/15/2001	food	12
7/22/2001	food	11	8/17/2001	food	11	9/16/2001	food	10
7/23/2001	food	10	8/18/2001	food	10	9/17/2001	food	9
7/24/2001	food	9	8/19/2001	food	10	9118/01	food	8
7/25/2001	food	10	8/20/2001	food	12	9/19/2001	school sp	23
7/26/2001	food	9	8/21/2001	food	10	9/19/2001	food	10
7/27/2001	movie	19	8/22/2001	food	10	9/20/2001	food	9
7/28/2001	clothes	68	8/23/2001	movie	18	9/21/2001	CD	13
7/29/2001	food	11	8/25/2001	school sp	19	9/22/2001	movie	19
7/30/2001	food	10	8/27/2001	food	8	9/23/2001	food	8
7/30/2001	food	8	8/28/2001	food	8	9/24/2001	food	7
7/31/2001	food	8	8/29/2001	food	9	9/25/2001	food	9
			8/30/2001	food	11	9/26/2001	food	10
						9/27/2001	food	9
						9/28/2001	food	10
						9/29/2001	school sp	18
						9/30/2001	food	10
Totals for month, by category								
You can use whatever headings, etc that you want to use.								

Assignment 3—Excel—Charts

For this next Excel assignment shown below, I asked the class to continue with the first project but add charts. I was not sure how the 4th grade would perform, but they did almost as well as the other grades. I had to explain charts and coordinates to the class but I believe that in general the class understood what we were doing.

History of My School Grades								
Course	Date	Grade	Date	Grade	Date	Grade	Date	Grade
	30-Sep		30-Oct		30-Nov		30-Dec	
Religion		90		85		85		92
Math		75		80		81		79
Science		78		80		80		78
Computer		85		82		82		85
Social Studies		87		83		81		86
Average		83		82		81.8		84

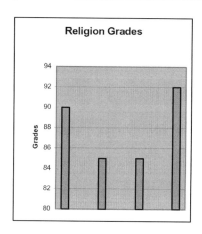

Column Chart

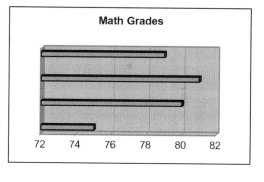

Bar Chart

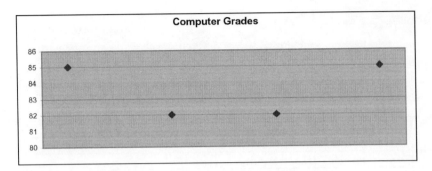

Line Chart

Excel Assignment 4—Excel Functions and Formulas

This assignment was given to the class to try just before Christmas. I added the "joke" of the extra gifts for me just to see what the students would say. Not one of the students told me that it was funny. I gave this assignment several weeks after the first Excel assignment and I soon discovered how quickly the students forgot formulas. I had to repeat all the instructions from the first Excel class in order for the class to complete this assignment.

Christmas Gifts		Gift	Price	
Mom		sweater	30	
Dad		dress shirt	25	
John		gloves	24	
Sam		scarf	19	
Mary		scarf	19	
Grandmother		gloves	23	
Hal		sweater	30	
Peter		shirt	22	
Susan		blouse	35	
Jamal		Tommy shirt	40	
Me		CD	23	
		sweater	40	
		blouse	45	
		blouse	40	
		CD	25	
		CD player	60	
		sweater	50	
			550	all gifts
			283	my gifts
			60	Most expensive gift
			19	Least Expensive

Excel Assignment 5—Monthly Expenses

This assignment is a continuation of a prior assignment. I added some new criteria for the students to play with. In order for the students to complete this assignment, I had to let them take the work home. The students just did not have enough time in class to complete the work assigned.

Monthly expense/ income								
Date	Expense	Amount	Total	Date	Income	Amount	Comment	Total
8/1/2001	food	8		8/3/2001	allowance	50		
8/5/2001	food	9		8/10/2001	allowance	50		
8/10/2001	movie	17		8/17/2001	allowance	50		
8/10/2001	clothes	68		8/17/2001	yard work	25		
8/11/2001	CD	13		8/24/2001	allowance	50		
8/15/2001	food	9		8/31/2001	allowance	50		275
8/17/2001	food	9		9/7/2001	allowance	50		
8/18/2001	food	10		9/14/2001	allowance	50		
8/20/2001	food	8		9/21/2001	allowance	50		
8/22/2001	food	9		9/28/2001	allowance	50		200
8/25/2001	movie	16						
8/27/2001	school	8						
8/29/2001	food	11	195					
9/2/2001	food	10						
9/3/2001	cd	16						
9/4/2001	food	9						
9/7/2001	movie	19						
9/10/2001	food	10						
9/11/2001	food	8						
9/12/2001	food	7						
9/14/2001	movie	16						
9/17/2001	food	9						
9/18/2001	food	9						
9/19/2001	food	8						
9/19/2001	clothes	55						
9/20/2001	food	6						
9/25/2001	food	8						
9/27/2001	food	8						
9/30/2001	food	11	209					
Total expense for August				195				
Total Income for August				275				
Amount left - August				80				
Total expense Sept				209				
Total income Sept				200				
Amount left - Sept				-9				

Amount of money spent during the month.
Amount of money left at end of month

Excel Assignment 6—World Trade Center Fund

The following is an Excel assignment that I gave to the class after the 9/11 disaster. This assignment contained clip art and additional functions. The assignments at this point became more difficult and in general, I only gave them to the seventh and eight grades. To verify that the students understood the assignment I insisted that they show me the formula they used to calculate the result.

Contributor		Amount		World Trade Center Fund		
				Month		Formula
Person A		$25.00		September		
Person A		$20.00		September		
Person B		$15.00		September		
Person B		$10.00		October		
Person B		$100.00		October		
Person C		$120.00		October		
Person D		$130.00		October		
Firm A		$4,000.00		September		
Firm B		$5,000.00		September		
Firm C		$40,000.00		November		
Firm D		$5,000.00		December		
Firm C		$5,500.00		December		
Firm D		$6,200.00		December		
Firm C		$5,400.00		January		
Firm D		$3,200.00		January		
Firm E		$1,560.00		February		
Firm E		$1,200.00		January		
Firm F		$1,500.00		January		
Firm G		$2,000.00		February		
Totals						
September		$9,060.00				
October		$360.00				
November		$40,000.00				
December		$16,700.00				

January		$11,300.00				
February		$3,560.00				
Total		$80,980.00				SUM(C12:C30)

INSTRUCTIONS

To receive full credit for this exercise you MUST:

Put your name and grade on the sheet
Show what formulas you used for the results (all totals)
Put the formula in the right hand column as I show for the final total
Use the correct fonts and BOLD as shown
Insert clip art if you
wish

Excel Assignment 7—Recipe

This exercise was the most difficult Excel assignment given to my class. I only used the assignment for the seventh and eight grades because it was far too difficult for the other classes to understand. The class was expected to enter the data as shown, using numeric edit as shown. The object of the assignment was to be able to modify the ingredients by changing the number of people that are staying for dinner. No one was able to figure out how to compute the new formula without assistance.

Four Bean Salad		Original				Modified
# of People		Formula				Formula
3	1.00	cup green beans			1.00	cup green beans
	1.50	cup red beans			1.50	cup red beans
	1.25	cup pinto beans			1.25	cup pinto beans
	1.00	cup chick peas			1.00	cup chick peas
	1.00	dash of parsley			1.00	dash of parsley
	1.00	teaspoon olive oil			1.00	teaspoon olive oil
Formula is for 3 people						
to modify amount of ingredients needed						
you just need to change the 3 (number of people in original recipe)						

to the new number of people.					
When you change the 3 the values in the new formula will change automatically.					
To receive full credit you MUST:					
Show the formula for the new results					
Show results to 2 decimal places					

The following are typing assignments that I assigned to the 4th and fifth grade. The intent was to let the students learn to type faster, compose better, to gain more experience with Word, and to think better. Even after many typing and writing assignments I noticed that in almost all classes, including the eighth grade, the students spelling and composition skills remained poor.

Assignment 8—Alien

Type your name, grade, and today's date on the top of the paper.

Your grade is based on the following instructions. The purpose of this assignment is:
- Learn to type faster
- Better composition skills
- Get you to think

You live on a planet far from earth in another solar system. Your planet has five moons and a binary star. You breathe carbon dioxide and expel oxygen. The planet consists of several very large bodies of land, which on your planet are called, trid. You only need a water type substance and light to survive.

Write at least three (3) paragraphs describing what you would look like and what life on your planet (call it planet X) is like.

The majority of the students gave very poor answers to this assignment. Most did not follow instructions, which was one of the objectives of the assignment. I also continued to notice how poor the student's composition and spelling skills were. Not one student noticed that the description I gave for the alien was for a plant and trid is dirt spelled backwards.

Assignment 9—Disabilities

This was a very interesting assignment that I decided to use because I am disabled. It was easy for the class to see my large external hearing aid, and many of the students commented on it. None of the students were malicious, they were just curious. To give them some insight into what it is like to have a disability, I asked them to type the following assignment.

<u>Type your name, grade, and today's date on the top of the paper.</u>

Your grade is based on following instructions.

Describe what it would be like, if you had a disability, such as being deaf or blind. How would you cope? How would you feel about yourself? How would you get along with others?

I felt that this was a very easy assignment but again the students were not very creative and all of the reports contained misspellings and grammatical errors.

Assignment 10—PowerPoint Assignment—The Holiday Season

The following assignment was used in the fourth through eight grades. It was used to reinforce their experience with PowerPoint.

Using presentation software Microsoft PowerPoint® create a presentation of the following:

Using slides, describe what any holiday season (July 4th, Christmas, Hanukah, Kwanzaa, New Year or some other holiday) means to you. Select one holiday only. You may use no more than two clip art pictures.

Instructions: You must put your name, grade and today's date on all pages. Print your slides before leaving. No more than four pages please.

All of the students selected Christmas and in general, they had a good time with the assignment. The only difficulty the students had was in sizing the clip art to fit the paper.

Assignment 11—Space Camp

Right after the Christmas recess I decided to get the students attention by introducing them to what I felt was an interesting topic, my two visits to Space Camp. I have always been interested in space, as a teenager I tried to build a rocket, therefore when Space Camp opened I had to go. I enjoyed the initial three-day program so much that I went back for a more extensive three-day program. For this assignment, I displayed the pictures of Space Camp, especially pertaining to the computers at mission control and on the orbiter, and then I asked the students to write a three-paragraph report on Space Camp. In most cases, the students did very poorly on this assignment. It did appear to me that they were interested in Space Camp but they paid more attention to the pictures than to what I was saying. One of the points of this exercise was my hope that I could generate some interest in science with some of the students. In at least one case that did happen. One of the girls in fifth grade was very interested in the pictures and my explanation and she asked many questions. I hope that this exercise leads her to a career path that she may not have felt confident enough before to try.

Assignment 12—PC Built-in Calculator Exercise

This assignment was similar to the calculator assignment that I presented to the third grade however; I made the example more difficult. No student was able to get question eight right. I don't know why they had trouble with this question but I did give them the solution.

PC Calculator Exercise 4th grade

NAME _____   GRADE _____

Using the built-in PC calculator complete the following exercise.

1. Add the following numbers.
    10
    3
    5
    6
    12   Answer _____

2. Subtract 134 from 241   Answer _____

3. Perform the following calculation:
    (123 + 456) – (45 – 12)   Answer _____

4. Perform the following calculation:
    a. (562 + 345 + 12 + 34) – 67   Answer _____

    b. 562 + 345 + 12 + 34 – 67   Answer _____

5. Perform the following calculation:
    (56 * 3) + 6   Answer _____

6. Perform the following calculation:
    (55/5) * 5   Answer _____

7. Perform the following calculation:
    (12 + 56 – 45 + 4) * 2   Answer _____

8. Perform the following calculation:
    (33/3) + 45 + (60 * 2)   Answer _____

9. Perform the following calculation:
    (44 * 2) + 10 – 8 – 2 + 10   Answer _____

10. Perform the following calculation:
    ((50 *2)/10) + (50 + 10 – 20)   Answer _____

Assignment 13—Computer Report

In order to improve the students experience with typing and the use of a report writing system (Word) and to give them some experience with research, I gave them the following project. The project was used for grades 4-8 however, the size requirements for the report changed. Listed below is the handout I gave for each of the grades. In general, the completed work was poor, and for the early grades 4-6, I was very generous with my marking.

The following is the handout used for the 4-6 grades.

Computer Report

Today, computers are used everywhere. They are used in cars, in appliances, in school, in stores, and in all types of machines. It is important to know about the history of computers so that you know how computers developed. It is important to know where computers are being used today in order to predict where computers will be in the future.

Your assignment is to examine at least two books in any library, and then write a one-page report on the early history of computers. Your report should be double spaced, margins on all sides 1", font Times New Roman, font style regular, and font size 12. At the end of your report, include the title and author for the two references, which you used.

You have three weeks to complete this assignment.

The following handout was modified and used for the seventh and eight grades.

Computer Report

Today, computers are used everywhere. They are used in cars, in appliances, in school, in stores, and in all types of machines. It is important to know about the history of computers so that you know how computers developed. It is important to know where computers are being used today in order to predict where computers will be in the future. Using this prior knowledge it might be possible to predict what computers might look like in the future. If you watch television or go to the movies, you can see that what people thought computers might look like in the future would already be obsolete today.

Your assignment is to examine at least three books in any library, and then write a three-page report on the history of computers and what you think computers might look like in 10 years. Your report should be double spaced, margins on all sides 1.25", font Times New Roman, font style regular, and font size 12. At the end of your report, include the title and author for the three references, which you used.

You have four weeks to complete this assignment.

Fifth and Sixth Grade

These grades also offered me a challenge. I wanted to expand on the lessons that I gave to the third and fourth grade but creating additional lessons was becoming more difficult. There are just so many assignments a teacher can create. The idea of teaching all of the early grades is difficult but the most difficult part is that you can't focus your assignments on just one age or grade. The teacher has to work hard to create many more lessons than would normally be expected. For these grades, I used many typing assignments. I was trying to expand their typing and Word skills but I also wanted them to think and be able to follow instructions.

The following was a handout used in the fifth and sixth grade to describe programming languages. I felt that it was important for the class to get a basic understanding of how languages are used and why programs need to be compiled or interpreted. The class however did not enjoy this discussion. I believe that it was too difficult for them to understand, and consequently I did not present the foils to the seventh and eight grades and I did not use the presentation again.

Programming Languages

Why do we need a programming language? Why can't we just talk to a computer?

- Computers cannot understand us.
- We need to convert how we speak and understand into what the computer can understand.
- We talk in words but the computer can only understand the numbers 1 and 0.

Computers translate our instructions into the numbers 1 and 0 so the computer can perform some function. This is done via a compiler, interpreter or assembler.

• Compilers—Convert and optimize an entire program into machine code.
• Assemblers—A compiler for assembler language.
• Interpreters—Convert English-like statements into machine code one statement at a time. An interpreted language program, such as Basic, runs much slower than a compiled language program, such as COBOL.

• FORTRAN—A language used for scientific programming. This is one of the early languages. This language is not used very much any more.
• Assembler—A language close to machine code. Programs written in Assembler run very fast.
ADA—This language is used it government. The government spent many years developing this language and programs now must be written in ADA.
• COBOL—Most common language used in business. Billions of dollars worth of programs have been created in COBOL. The programs created in COBOL were the programs that many people felt would fail during the Y2K scare.
• PL1—Early language but not used much today.
• Basic—Early PC based language. A very easy to learn language that is not readily available anymore. Visual Basic has replaced Basic. Basic was originally invented because people thought that COBOL and FORTRAN were too difficult to learn.
• C and C++ - C was an early language used on UNIX machines. C++ is a more modern version of C.
• Java—Modern language used for web development. This is a very popular language but is not very easy to use. It is similar to C++.

• Script Languages
• TML
• JavaScript
• Pearl

The following is a handout that I gave to all students from sixth through eight grades. In some cases, the students already knew most of what is contained in the handout but in many cases, the handout was very useful. This handout could be used as a discussion topic before you build a web site (see *Building a Class Web Site*).

The Web

The World Wide Web (WWW, W3, or just the Web) is a recent innovation that will make school, work, and play easier and more fun. It will make school easier because you can do research for your assignments from your computer. You will be able to obtain interesting and up-to-date information on many subjects. You may want to explore new subjects just because it is easy to do. However, what exactly is the Web?

The World Wide Web is part of the Internet. The Web consists of a huge collection of documents stored on computers around the world. The World Wide Web is also called the Web or WWW. A Web site is a collection of Web Pages maintained by a college, university, government agency, company or individual. Each Web page has a unique address, called the Uniform Resource Locator (URL). You can instantly display the Web page if you know its URL. Most Web pages start with http, which stands for Hypertext Transfer Protocol. If you do not know the URL for a Web page, you can use a search engine to find it. A search engine, such as Yahoo or Goggle, contains a large list of Web Page URL's. When you perform a search using some key word, the search engine will perform a search to see which web pages contain those key words in its HTML code. All HTML code should contain some key words that will allow someone to find your Web Page. This is usually done by including some form of the META statement in your code. When you use an HTML editor, these statements will be created for you. A typical HTML statement is; <B> This is an HTML statement</B>. The <B> and </B> are *tags* that tell the interpreter to mark the text within those statements as **bold** text.

Hypertext Markup Language (HTML) is the computer code used to create Web pages. There are many programs available, called HTML editors, which can be used to create Web pages without learning this language.

A browser is the software that allows you to view and surf different Web sites. Most computers use either Netscape or Microsoft Internet Explorer as a browser. Both are available free and one or both come with all computers. AOL subscribers often use the AOL browser that comes with AOL, though you can also use Netscape or Explorer with AOL.

Seventh and Eight Grade

Because the eight grade had to take assessment exams, I tried to include as many examples of this type of assessment in my classes as possible. These assignments would give the students knowledge on computer topics as well as more experience in typing and on how to take the assessment test. The following are several assessments that I developed for the class. I did all the research for the tests and the typing of the tests. I find it most effective to use handouts in class, especially handouts that are neatly typed.

For both the seventh and eight grades, the class was required to type the answers to the assessment in class using Word. I modified the font and size requirements for each of the tests.

Assessment Exam 1—History of Computers

This question is based on the accompanying documents (1-5). Some of the documents have been edited for the purpose of the question. The question is designed to test your ability to work with documents related to computer history. As you analyze the documents, take into account both the content of each document and any point of view that may be presented in the document.

Directions: Using the document, the answers to the questions in Part A, and your knowledge of computer history, write, in Word, a well-organized essay about the role of computers in modern society. You should use a font of 14, font type of Times New Roman, margins of 1.25" for top and bottom, and 1" on both sides.

In your essay, remember to:
- Tell about the early history of computers before World War II and after.
- Include an introduction, body, and conclusion
- Include details, examples, or reasons in developing your ideas
- Use the information from the documents in your answer

Computer Background: Computers have played a very important role (part) in society. Like most other major inventions, many previous inventions affected the growth of the use of computers.

Task:

For Part A, read each document carefully and answer the questions after each document. These answers will help you write your essay. Then read the directions for Part B and write your essay.

Part A
Short—Answer Questions

Directions: Read each document and answer the question or questions that follow each document by typing your answer in Word. *Be sure your name, grade and today's date are on the Word document.*

Document 1

Computers are not a recent invention. Very early computers include the abacus, which was invented in Asia in 500 BC. The abacus is an adding machine using beads and strings. It is still in use today. The oldest known computing device is a tally stick made from the shinbone of a wolf. They are known to be from the Stone Age, going back at least 5,000 years B.C. Another early "computer" was a hand-held device that was used to help with multiplication and division. This device was invented around 1600 by John Napier and was called Napier's Bones. In 1622, William Oughtred invented the slide rule, based on the logarithms invented by Napier. Other early uses of computers (a machine that computes) include a primitive adding machine, invented by a French scientist, Pascal, in 1642 and a punched card machine, invented in 1801 by Joseph Jacquard, used to make rugs. Pascal's machine included wheels with numbers on them, causing gears to mesh and totals to be displayed. Another early computer was an analytical engine built in 1830 by an English inventor, Babbage. Babbage spent 40 years designing a machine that he called the analytical engine. This machine used stored punched cards to remember data and instructions. This invention was far ahead of its time and was not used because no one could find a use for it until many years later.

1. Early "computers" were used for practical purposes. Contrast (tell the difference) the purposes (uses) of two of the early computers.

Document 2

During World War II, the allies needed a way to decipher the secret codes of the enemy. The computer invented by England to decipher this code was called *Colossuss 1.*

The allies also needed a better way to calculate the trajectory (path) of missiles so that they could be more accurate. As a result of these military needs, large computers were invented. These computers were slow compared to today's computers and very large. The computers could fill a large room. They also used mechanical components to perform computations. Early computers also could not run if the temperature or humidity rose too high.

1. What caused the development of modern computers?
2. Do you think that modern computers would have been invented if not for the military's needs? Give your reason.

Document 3

Several early post World War II computers were the ENIAC (Electronic Numerical Integrator and Computer), which contained 19,000 triodes (glass tubes) and weighed 30 tons, the EDVAC and the UNIVAC. The UNIVAC was the first "mass-produced" computer. These computers used vacuum tubes in place of mechanical parts. Although this made the computer faster, the large number of tubes made the computer heavy and caused the computer to overheat. The tubes also blew out often. These early computers were so large that they could not fit in a large garage. One early use of these computers was to report election results.

Picture of an early large computer.

1. Why were the first computers so large and heavy?

Document 4

Large-scale computes began to be widely used in business in the late 1950's and early 1960's. Corporations found that as they grew they could not handle the large volume of data and reports that needed to be produced. A better way, other than hiring many more people, had to be found. Early computers were each unique. When a company grew and they needed a larger or more powerful computer the company needed to rewrite all their programs and reformat their data to suit the requirements of the new computer. In the early 1960's IBM released a family of machines called the System 360 family. The IBM series of System 360 machines made it very easy for companies to buy a small machine, and when a company became larger, transfer its data to the next larger size System 360 without having to rewrite the code. This series of computers and the concept of a series of next step larger machines was revolutionary and enabled IBM to become dominate for many years.

1. Why was one company able to dominate the compute field for so long?

Document 5

Although computers had been in use for 20 years, they had not been used successfully in the home. Most people felt that they did not need a computer at home. In fact, the president of IBM felt that only a handful of personal computers would ever be needed and sold. This perception changed with the invention of the first Apple computer and the software spreadsheet software, VisiCalc. Computers were now small enough to be used at home and VisiCalc could be used to perform many household and business calculations. Although the Apple computer was the first family computer, when the IBM PC was introduced it soon became the computer of choice. This had a lot to do with the IBM name, but also with the DOS operation system that ran on the IBM PC. The IBM PC and clones (IBM type PC's) quickly became the dominant computer at home and in the office. When Microsoft introduced its suite of products, such as Word and Excel; PC's were no longer novelties but became an appliance that everyone had to have. PC's are now in almost as many homes as TV's. Because of the relative low cost of PC's, it is possible for most families to have at least one PC at home.

 Personal Computer

1. Why did the IBM PC become the dominant PC?

Part B

For Part B use the information from the documents, your answers in Part A, and your knowledge of computers to write a well-organized essay. In the essay, you should:

> Write about the growth of computers and their impact on society.

Students: For more information on this topic, visit the Computer History Museum on-line at http://www.computerhistory.org.

This second history of computers assessment test was given to the students in the 7th and 8th grades to help build more confidence in the students regarding the history assessment test that they would be taking. In addition the test gave them more knowledge about the history of computers.

Assessment Exam 2—History of Computers Part 2

This question is based on the accompanying documents (1-5). Some of the documents have been edited for the purpose of the question. The question is designed to test your ability to work with documents related to computer history. As you analyze the documents, take into account both the contents of each document and any point of view that may be presented in the document.

Directions: Using the document, the answers to the questions in Part A, and your knowledge of computer history, write, in Word, a well-organized essay about the role of computers in modern society. Include your name, today's date and your grade (7th or 8th) on the first page. You should use a font of 12, font type of Arial, margins of 1.25" for top and bottom, and 1" on both sides.

In your essay, remember to:

- Tell about the history of computers and how so many countries became responsible for the development of the computer.
- Include an introduction, body, and conclusion
- Include details, examples, or reasons in developing your ideas
- Use the information from the documents in your answer

Computer Background: Computers have played a very important role (part) in society. Like most other major inventions, many previous inventions affected the growth of the use of computers. Many countries also contributed to the development of the computer.

Task:

For Part A, read each document carefully and answer the questions after each document. These answers will help you write your essay. Then read the directions for Part B and write your essay.

Part A
Short—Answer Questions

Directions: Read each document and answer the question or questions that follow each document by typing your answer in Word. *Be sure your name, grade and today's date is on the Word document.*

Document 1

Computers are not a recent invention. Many of the earliest methods of recording and counting data are shrouded in mystery. In England, you can visit Stonehenge, where a mysterious collection of large stones has stood since 1,500 B.C. Scientists have never discovered the stones purpose. However, by observing the way the sun shines between the stones, many people believe Stonehenge was used to predict the seasons and eclipses of the sun and moon. In early-recorded history, calculators that used the sun, or objects in the night sky were developed to help early navigators explore the word beyond the Tigris-Euphrates Valley of southwestern Asia. Very early computers include the abacus invented in Asia in 500 BC. The abacus is an adding machine using beads and strings. It is still in use today.

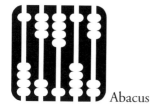 Abacus
 Stonehenge

1. What were early "computers" or calculating devices used for?

Document 2

Other early uses of computers (a machine that computes) include a primitive adding machine, invented by a French scientist, Pascal, in 1642 and a punched card machine, invented in 1801 by Joseph Jacquard, used to make rugs. Another early computer was an analytical engine invented in 1830 by an English inventor, Babbage. Babbage spent 40 years designing a machine that he called the analytical engine. This machine used stored punched cards to remember data and instructions. This invention was far ahead of its time and was not used because no one could find a use for it until many years later. The idea of the analytical engine would have been lost if it were not for a women who worked with Babbage. Lady Ada Byron wrote down everything that Babbage planned for the machine. She also wrote out detailed mathematical steps the "engine" would follow to solve a problem. Because of her work, many people consider Lady Byron the first computer programmer. The ADA programming language is named for her.

1. Why do we know about Babbage's invention today after all these years?

Document 3

Around the turn of the century Herman Hollerith, a young man who worked for the U.S. Bureau of the Census, came up with an idea that greatly changed the way business kept records. In those days census counts were done by hand with the aid of some adding and bookkeeping machines. It was a never-ending job. Many times the counting was not finished before the next census was taken ten years later. The census of 1880 took over seven years to complete. Hollerith came up with the same approach for storing information as Jacquard had used with his loom. He stored information on small cards that could be used for adding, subtracting and printing. Instead of printing information on the cards, he recorded the information by punching holes in the cards. Each hole represented a different number. Once information was punched in the cards, machines could use the cards for calculations. This invention enabled the census to be completed in two and a half years instead of seven years like the previous census. The punched card was also the start of the American computer revolution.

1. How did Hollerith's invention improve census taking?

Document 4

When World War II broke out, the need for up-to-date information grew quickly. Several reasons were; the movement of millions of soldiers had to be tracked, new ways to send information over telephone lines in code had to be accomplished, and new weapons needed to be designed. There was a rush to build machines that could give answers faster than punched card systems could. An early computer developed in England, and designed by Alan Turing was called

Colossus. This machine helped decipher the German secret code and helped win the war for the allies. Alan Turing also devised a test, called the Turing test, to see if a computer could be considered to be human. The test went like this: first, place a computer with a computer operator in one room and a person in another room. Next, ask the computer and the person questions. If you can't tell which is the computer and which is the human, then the computer has passed the Turing test. To this date, no computer has passed this test.

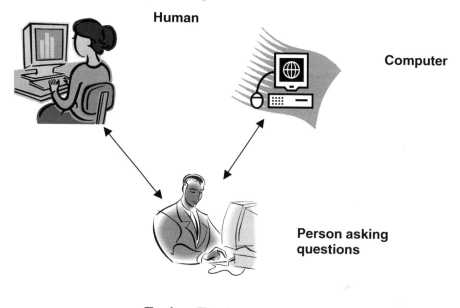

Human

Computer

Person asking questions

Turing Test

1. What reasons can you give for the need for a new type of computer other than a punched card system?
2. Has any computer ever been mistaken for a human?

Document 5

Another contributor to the development of computers was John von Neumann. He invented a computer that used its memory to store instructions or program steps. Instead of rewiring the computer for each new job, program steps or instructions could be read into memory. This design allowed the same computer to be set up for a new problem in only minutes. Most of today's computers are designed the same way as the von Neumann machines. This type of computer allows people to write programs, which are just a series of instructions, which is understandable to the computer. All computers today use memory to store instructions.

1. How did the von Neumann computer differ from earlier computers?

Part B

For Part B, use the information from the documents, your answers in Part A, and your knowledge of computers to write a well-organized essay. In the essay, you should:

Write about the growth of computers.

Students: For more information on this topic, visit the Computer History Museum on-line at http://www.computerhistory.org.

The following assessment was used to give the students more experience with the social studies test. This test concerned the history of the Internet. Most of the students already used the Internet but I wanted them to understand where the Internet came from and how it developed, not just what web sites to use.

Assessment Exam 3—History of the Internet

This question is based on the accompanying documents (1-6). Some of the documents have been edited for the purpose of the question. The question is designed to test your ability to work with documents related to the history of the Internet. As you analyze the documents, take into account both the content of each document and any point of view that may be presented in the document.

Directions: Using the document, the answers to the questions in Part A, and your knowledge of the Internet, write, in Word, a well-organized essay about the history of the Internet. Include your name, today's date and your grade (7th or 8th) on the first page. You should use a font of 12, font type of Arial, margins of 1.25" for top and bottom, and 1" on both sides.

In your essay, remember to:
- Tell about the early history of the Internet.
- Include an introduction, body, and conclusion
- Include details, examples, or reasons in developing your ideas
- Use the information from the documents in your answer.

Internet Background: The Internet is often called the net, the information super-highway or cyberspace. Because of safeguards built into the design of the Internet, if part of the Internet fails, information finds a new route around the disabled computers.

Task:

For Part A, read each document carefully and answer the questions after each document. These answers will help you write your essay. Then read the directions for Part B and write your essay.

Part A
Short—Answer Questions

Directions: Read each document and answer the question or questions that follow each document by typing your answer in Word. Be sure your name, date, and grade are on the Word document.

Document 1

In the late 1960's the U.S. Defense Department began the Internet. This project was originally called the ARPANET (**A**dvanced **R**esearch **P**rojects **A**gency **N**etwork).The Internet was developed by the US Defense Department to allow different agencies to continue to operate even if part of the network were to fail. The Internet is designed to be unreliable, that is, any portion of the network could fail, but the rest of the network would still operate. This is because information would be rerouted around the failing part of the Internet. The Internet quickly grew to include scientists and researchers across the country and eventually schools, businesses, libraries and individuals around the world.

1. Why was the Internet originally developed?

Document 2

The Internet consists of thousands of connected networks around the world. A network is a collection of computers that are connected to share information. Each government company and organization on the Internet is responsible for maintaining its own network. There is no centralized management of the Internet. Each of the networks is run on its own. Each network cooperates with the other networks to direct Internet traffic so that information can pass among them. Together, these networks and organizations make up the Internet. When a business creates its company web page, the web page must be stored somewhere so that it can be accessed by others. This ability to access a company's network via the web is what makes hacking so popular. Hacking involves illegally accessing an organizations files. Many times this can be accomplished by using a company's web site. People with computer skills try to access a company's web site in order to gain access to the company's network. This can allow them to change the company's web site or to search for company's files, or worse, to infect the company's files with a virus or bug. Because of these security issues, many companies install hardware and software to restrict or limit access to company files. This hardware and software is usually called a firewall.

1. What is a network?
2. Who maintains an organization's network on the Internet?

Document 3

The World Wide Web (WWW) began as a networked project from the European Particle Physics Laboratory. It was originally created as a way for physicists to share information about their research. The World Wide Web is part of the Internet. The Web consists of a huge collection of documents stored on computers around the world. The World Wide Web is also called the Web or WWW. A Web site is a collection of Web Pages maintained by a college, university, government agency, company or individual. Today the Web is used by people to share and access all types of data, from reports to music to film. Many people feel that the Web will be the primary means of communicating in the future. It is already one of the primary ways today that people find information and it will one day be the primary way that people will shop.

1. If you create your own home page with information about yourself and then make it available to others, is your home page considered a web site? Why?

Document 4

Each Web page has a unique address, called the Uniform Resource Locator (URL). You can instantly display the Web page if you know its URL. Most Web pages start with http, which stands for Hypertext Transfer Protocol. A Web page can include text (words), pictures, vocals (speech or music) and links to other Web pages. A link to another page or to a location on the same page is called a hyperlink. A Web site can consist of one page or many pages. The Web site can be for a business, a school or for a person. Anyone can create their own Web site and make it available to view by others. Even though information is on the Web that does not mean the information is correct. Anyone can post information on the Web and when searching for information people should examine where the information comes from before assuming that the information is correct.

1. What is the difference between an URL and http?

Document 5

Hypertext Markup Language (HTML) is the computer code used to create Web pages. There are many programs available, called HTML editors, which can be used to create Web pages without learning HTML. Some HTML editors include FrontPage, Microsoft Word, and DreamWeaver. HTML is a simple language to learn and to use but it does require some programming experience. A sample of an HTML statement is <B>Sample Text</B>. The <B> asks the computer to make the following text bold, the </B> statement tells the computer to stop making text bold. The <B> and </B> are called *tags*. Although a Web page created by HTML can display almost anything, if you want to use automation (pictures or text that moves) you would need to use a specialized language such as Java. Java was not originally created for the Web but was instead created to run appliances such as refrigerators. Today Java is used to run many appliances and to write Web applications.

1. Explain two ways that you can use to create a web page.

Document 6

A browser is the software that allows you to view and surf different Web sites. Most computers use either Netscape or Microsoft Internet Explorer as a browser. Both are available free and one or both come with all computers. AOL subscribers often use the AOL browser that comes with AOL, though you can also use Netscape or Explorer with AOL. A search engine, such as Yahoo and Google, can be used to search the Internet for information based on a word or words that a person types. The search engine uses a complex algorithm and key words to find the documents you are looking for. Most people, who have web sites, want their web site to be found, therefore they pay these search engine firms a fee in order for their web site to be listed at the top of a successful search. The Internet Service Providers (ISP's) are companies that sell customers monthly access to the Internet. An example of an ISP is EarthLink.

1. What is a web browser?
2. What is a search engine?

Part B

For Part B, use the information from the documents, your answers in Part A, and your knowledge of the Internet to write a well-organized essay. In the essay, you should:

> Write about the history of the Internet and the Web and the differences between the parts of the web such as browsers, URL's, etc.

Students: For more information on this topic, please visit web site http://www.isoc.org/internet/history/brief.shtml.

The following math assessment test was given to the seventh and eight grades to take and for the fifth and sixth grades to type. This is a very good typing exercise because of all the special characters. I split the test into three parts. One day I gave the first five questions, another day I gave the next five questions and then I gave the remaining questions. Feel free to see if you can do the math. I can tell you that no one in either the seventh or eight grades got even the first five questions right. Everyone missed the second question and no one could do question three or four. To me this is a sad commentary on what we are teaching children today. In my opinion, there is no way that seventh and eight grade students could not do these questions. Because so many students failed to complete the questions, I decided to type the solutions to some of the questions and hand them out to the class. Many students did not seem interested in learning what they did wrong or how to do the problems. This was going to affect them and the school when they took the exam later in the year.

Assessment Exam 4—Math

Complete the following math questions. Type, in WORD, your NAME, GRADE and today's date on the top of the page. Show all work (how you came up with your answer)

The NYS Math test consists of:
Session 1
Part 1 (35 minutes) 27 multiple choice questions (1 point)
Part 2 (35 minutes) 4 short response questions (0-2 points)
                    2 extended-response questions (0-3 points)
Session 2 (70 minutes)
8 short response questions (0-2 points)
4 extended-response questions (0-3 points)

1. A teacher is making 7 different walking sticks for use in a school play. If each stick requires 3 ¾ feet of wood, how much wood is needed altogether for the seven walking sticks?
    a.   10 ¾
    b.   17 ½
    c.   21 ¾
    d.   26 ¼

2. Kerry and her mother used 45 feet of rope from a 60 yard bundle of rope. How many feet of rope were left in the bundle?
    a.   15 feet
    b.   60 feet
    c.   105 feet
    d.   135 feet

3. Terrence is thinking of a number greater than 150 and less than 200, and Juanita has to guess it, He has provided Juanita with the following clue—the number is divisible by 2, 3 and 5. What number is Terrence thinking of?
    a.   150
    b.   160
    c.   180
    d.   195

4. The variables q,x,y and z each represent a different whole number. If you know that q = 4, use the properties of whole numbers to determine the numerical value for each of the remaining variables. Show all of your work.

$q * y = q$

$z + 2y = q$

$z * x = x$

$y + y = z$

x =   y =   z =

5. Due to increased demand, a car dealership recently raised the price on its new convertibles by 36%. If the original cost of a convertible was $26,935, what is the new cost, after the increase?
    a. $74,819.44
    b. $36,631.60
    c. $26,971.00
    d. $9,696.60

6. Several students have joined to make a pot of clam chowder for their class. Each student has a recipe that calls for different amounts of clams to be used. The following is a list of the various amounts of clams, in pounds, that each recipe calls for.

    2 ¼
    8/3
    2 1/8
    2.5
    2 1/3

    The students want to use the largest number of clams. Which amount should they use?
    Explain how you determined which number was largest.

7. The ratio of students to teachers at Middlebrook High School is 7 to 4. If there are 28 teachers at the school, how many students are there?
    a. 16
    b. 28
    c. 49
    d. 196

8. A rectangular park is 110 yards long and 43 2/3 yards wide. If a person walked all the way around the outside edge of the park, how many yards would they walk?

a. 153 2/3 yards
b. 197 1/3 yards
c. 263 2/3 yards
d. 307 1/3 yards

9. For one week, a clothing store kept track of the number of customers it had during the week. What is the mean number of customers for that five-day period?

Monday   140
Tuesday   90
Wednesday   250
Thursday   140
Friday   70

a. 98
b. 138
c. 140
d. 250

10. Create an Excel spreadsheet of the days and numbers for question 10. Also, create a bar graph for these values.

11. Theodore is monitoring the growth of fast-growing algae. He has discovered that the algae cells reproduce by dividing in half every forty minutes.

Part A. If Theodore starts out with 2 algae cells, how many cells will there be in 4 hours? Show your work.
Part B. After how many minutes will there be 1,024 algae cells? Show your work.

14. Diana wrote the following facts about three different numbers: a, b, c

Fact 1: $a/c = a$
Fact 2: $a + b = a$
Fact 3: $abc = 1$

Part A: If Fact 1 and Fact 2 are true, explain why Fact 3 is NOT true.
Part B: What are the values of each of the variables in Fact 1 and Fact 2?

a =
b =
c =

15. Kyle says that he can pick any number between 1 and 100, add 1 to it, multiply the result by 2, add 2 to that result, then subtract 2 times the number he started with, and he will always get the same answer (the number he started with).

Using x to represent any number between 1 and 100, write an expression that demonstrates the process described above.

Is Kyle correct? Explain why or why not.

16. Using the following numbers:
6.25
-3 ¾
1.5^2
-0.5
$\sqrt{81}$
18/4

Put these numbers in order from smallest to largest.

17. a. List all the whole numbers from one to 100 that can be evenly divided by both 6 and 15.

b. Describe at least one pattern that you notice in your answer.
c. How many whole numbers between 290 and 410 can be evenly divided by both 6 and 15? Show your work.

18. What number should come next in this pattern?
1,2,2,4,8,32,

a. 16
b. 64
c. 126
d. 256

19. A recipe for a pot of gumbo calls for 4/5 cup of okra to make 8 bowls of gumbo. How many cups of okra would be needed to make 10 pots of gumbo?
    a.   4/5 cups
    b.   8 cups
    c.   10 cups
    d.   12 ½ cups

20. In the expression below, insert two sets of parentheses so that the expression is equal to 12. Show the steps you used to simplify the expression to show that it equals 12. Show your work.

$$\frac{4 * 15 + 2\,^2 - 4}{3 - 2 * 6}$$

The following is the handout that I gave the students with the solutions to several questions. I gave the answers to the students not only because they did so poorly on the assessment quiz but also because these questions were the type of questions that they could expect to see on the test. I do not know if the students read the answers but I did explain the answers in class in order for them to have just a little bit of knowledge on how to do the problems and what they did wrong. These questions were actual questions from previous tests.

Math Assessment Answers

The following are the answers to the math questions that you tried to complete in class. When you take this test, the best suggestion that I can give is to relax. Also READ the question. Eliminate obvious wrong answers then solve for the answer.

1.   A teacher is making 7 different walking sticks for use in a school play. If each stick requires 3 ¾ feet of wood, how much wood is needed altogether for the seven walking sticks?
    e.   10 ¾
    f.   17 ½
    g.   21 ¾
    h.   26 ¼

Answer: If each stick is to be 3 ¾ feet and you need 7 then just multiply 7 * 3 ¾
7/1 * 15/4 = 105/4 = 26 ¼, therefore the answer is d.

2. Kerry and her mother used 45 feet of rope from a 60 yard bundle of rope. How many feet of rope were left in the bundle?
    e. 15 feet
    f. 60 feet
    g. 105 feet
    h. 135 feet

Be careful of these types of questions because they are used to trick you and they are often on the test. Before you can solve this, you must convert yards to feet. Since there are 3 feet in a yard, you should multiple 60 by 3 to get 180 feet. Now you can subtract 45 feet from 180 feet to get the answer 135 feet.

3. Terrence is thinking of a number greater than 150 and less than 200, and Juanita has to guess it, He has provided Juanita with the following clue-the number is divisible by 2, 3 and 5. What number is Terrence thinking of?
    a. 150
    b. 160
    c. 180
    d. 195

You can use a technique similar to lowest common denominator and lowest common multiplier that you learned in 4th grade to solve this example. Multiply 2 by 3 by 5 to get the lowest common multiplier, which is 30. Which of the answers do 30 go into? Only 180 so that is your answer.

4. The variables q, x, y and z each represent a different whole number. If you know that q = 4, use the properties of whole numbers to determine the numerical value for each of the remaining variables. Show all of your work.

$q * y = q$

$z + 2y = q$

$z * x = x$

$y + y = z$

x =   y =   z =

This question is not as hard as it looks. Just solve one equation after another to get the answer as in the following:
First, substitute what you know into the first equation.
$4 * y = 4$ The only number that you can multiply 4 by to get 4 is 1 so y must be 1.
$Z + 2(1) = 4$ when you solve this equation you get z = 2

2 * x = x What number can you multiply by 2 to get back the original number? Only 0 fits so x = 0.
1 + 1 = 2. This last equation is the proof that you are correct.

5. Due to increased demand, a car dealership recently raised the price on its new convertibles by 36%. If the original cost of a convertible was $26,935, what is the new cost, after the increase?
    a. $74,819.44
    b. $36,631.60
    c. $26,971.00
    e. $9,696.60

If the car cost $26,935 and you raise the price by 36% what is the new price? Multiply the original price by 36% to get $9,696.60. Add the increase to the original cost to get the answer $36,631.60.

6. For this question the best thing to do is use the Less Common Denominator (LCD) process as follows. First convert each of the numbers to a fraction; so 2 ¼ would be 9/4, 2.5 would be 5/2 etc. You would now be left with the following fractions:
    9/4 8/3 17/8 5/2 7/3. You now need a LCD. What number can 4, 3, 8 and 2 go into? The answer is 24. How did I get 24? Two goes into 4 so you do not need the 2. Four goes into eight so you do not need the four. You are now left with the three and eight. Multiply the eight by three to get 24. Convert all of the fractions to a new fraction with a denominator of 24 and you will have 72/24 64/24 51/24 60/24 56/24. The largest number is 72/24 or 2 ¼.

7. A ratio means as a is related to b then c is related to d. Watch how this works for this question. There are 7 students for 4 teachers so 7 is to 4. Now if there are 28 total teachers how many students are there? You put all the numbers together as follows: 7 is to 4 as x is to 28. This reads as 7:4::x:28. To solve for x first multiply 28 by 7 to get 196. Now multiply the 4 by x to get 4x, you are left with 4x=196. Solve for x by dividing 196 by 4 and you get 49, so the correct answer is c.

This next test, like the previous tests, was used to prepare the students to take the real assessment test. I felt that a discussion on robots might hold the student's attention. In general, it did not. Students quickly became bored with taking the tests and usually performed poorly on them.

Assessment Test 5—Robots Part I

This question is based on the accompanying documents (1-5). Some of the documents have been edited for the purpose of the question. The question is designed to test your ability to work with documents related to the early history of robots. As you analyze the documents, take into account both the content of each document and any point of view that may be presented in the document.

Directions: Using the document, the answers to the questions in Part A, and your knowledge of robotics, type a well-organized essay about the role of robots in pre 20th century. Include your name, today's date and your grade (7th or 8th) on the first page. You should use a font of 12, font type of Arial, margins of 1.25" for top and bottom, and 1" on both sides.

In your essay, remember to:
- Tell about the history of robots and how so many countries used robots for fun or to perform some work.
- Include an introduction, body, and conclusion
- Include details, examples, or reasons in developing your ideas
- Use the information from the documents in your answer to complete Part B.

Robotics Background: Robots have played a very important role (part) in society. Like most other major inventions, many previous inventions affected the growth and use of robots. Many countries also contributed to the development of the modern robot.

Task:

For Part A, read each document carefully and answer the questions after each document. These answers will help you write your essay. Then read the directions for Part B and write your essay.

Part A
Short—Answer Questions

Directions: Read each document and answer the question or questions that follow each document by typing your answer.

Document 1

The following are definitions, which will help in your understanding of the topic of robots. A robot is generally a mechanical apparatus doing the work of a human being. A robot does not have to look human but must be able to perform some human actions and functions. An automaton is a mechanical figure or contrivance constructed to act as if by its own motive power. A humanoid is a machine or robot, which has human characteristics in its physical appearance. An android is an automaton or robot that is human in appearance and may, in fact, duplicate some actions and functions of the human body.

An Android

1. What is the basic difference between a humanoid and an android?
2. What is the difference between a robot and an android?

Document 2

As far back as 2000 years ago, water powered automation figures struck bells at scheduled intervals to help Egyptians keep track of time. Around 200 B.C., Hero of Alexander designed and built complicated, elaborate, and amusing automata. He made a steam-powered merry-go-round and a hydraulically powered statue of Hercules slaying a dragon. About 600 years ago, the Chinese used a robot patient to train doctors in the use of acupuncture. The trainee inserted the acupuncture needles into the robot patient, a life-size bronze figure. If the needle were inserted correctly, the robot patient would squirt water out of the needle hole. Although none of these devices looked human, they did perform some automatic function.

Acupuncture

1. What is the difference between the "robot" devices of the Chinese and the devices that Hero of Alexander created?

Document 3

Some early forms of automata are listed below and show how complex they were for their day.

Complex automata appeared in Europe about 600 years ago. Albertus Magnus, a Bavarian philosopher, spent twenty years constructing an automaton. This automaton could move toward a door, answer it, and then salute the visitor. The story goes that when St. Thomas Aquinas saw the automaton he denounced it as the work of the devil and smashed it beyond repair.

Leonardo da Vinci, the Italian genius, made a mechanical walking lion.

Other automaton were the many clocks in large cathedrals of Europe that had moving parts that strike bells, move and perform other gyrations when telling time. The cuckoo clock, which appeared around 1730, is an automata with singing or musical devices.
Another automata was Jacques de Vaucanson's artificial copper duck displayed in 1738.
This "duck" could drink, eat, quack, splash around in the water, digest its food and voided. The duck was eventually sold and was seen at the famous opera house in Milan Italy. Eventually the duck disappeared and to this day, no one knows what happen to the artificial duck or how it was able to "digest" food.

1. Could any of the automata described above in Document 3 be considered a robot? Why or why not?

Document 4

Soon new automata began to appear. These included mechanical writers. One of the first was one made by Fredrick Von Knaus. One of these mechanical writers had a small figure on top of the mechanism. The figure would write passages of various lengths. The figure also dipped its pen into an inkwell to replenish the pen's ink supply. Another mechanical writer, by Pierre Jacquet-Droz and his son consisted of a very life-like figure of a boy. This figure would dip his pen in an inkwell, shake the pen twice, pause then begin to write. This device can be seen today in a Swiss museum. These writing automata were only the beginning of performing robots. Other automata included devices that danced, sang, walked and played musical instruments. These devices were remarkable for their time.

1. What devices today are similar to the mechanical writers and in what way are they somewhat different?

Document 5

The "Chess Player" developed by Baron Wolfgang Von Kempelen was one of the most famous performing robots. The "Chess Player" was a large box-like structure with a chessboard on top. Behind the chessboard was the figure of a man. This device was built to play chess against real people and in fact usually won. Although never proved, it appeared that there was a person in the "Chess Player" machine making the moves. Although Von Kempelen's "Chess Player" was probably a fraud, he did develop the first true automaton that could talk. It reproduced human speech through the use of air pipes.

Another robot was made by J.N. Malkelyne in the 1870's. This robot, called Psyco, could: nod, shake hands, solve mathematical problems, smoke and perform magical tricks. It was also very good at playing, and winning at cards.

1. How did the "Chess Player" differ from the "Psyco" robot?

Part B

For Part B, use the information from the documents, your answers in Part A, and your knowledge of robots to write a well-organized essay. In the essay you should:

Write about the early uses of robots.

Students: For more information on this topic, visit the following web site and the other links available from this web site http://www.neuroprosthesis.org/bbook.htm.

This second assessment test on robots was used as an extension of the first robot assessment test. The students may not have wanted to take the tests but I felt the students might be interested in learning about robots and similar types of devices. Creating these tests was becoming more difficult because I had to research the information and then type the tests. I was willing to make the effort because I knew that the experience was helping the students.

Assessment Test 6—Robots Part II

This question is based on the accompanying documents (1-6). Some of the documents have been edited for the purpose of the question. The question is designed to test your ability to work with documents related to the history of robots in the 20th century. As you analyze the documents, take into account both the content of each document and any point of view that may be presented in the document.

Directions: Using the document, the answers to the questions in Part A, and your knowledge of robotics, write, in Word, a well-organized essay about the role of robots in the 20th century. Include your name, today's date and your grade on the first page. You should use a font size of 12, font of Arial Black, margins of 1.5 on all four sides.

In your essay, remember to:
- Tell about the history of robots in the 20th century and how robots were used and may be used in the future.
- Include an introduction, body, and conclusion
- Include details, examples, or reasons in developing your ideas
- Use the information from the documents in your answer

Robotics Background: Robots have played a very important role (part) in society. Like most other major inventions, many previous inventions affected the growth and use of robots. Many countries also contributed to the development of the modern robot.

Task:

For Part A, read each document carefully and answer the questions after each document. These answers will help you write your essay. Then read the directions for Part B and write your essay.

Part A
Short—Answer Questions

Directions: Read each document and answer the question or questions that follow each document by typing your answer in Word. *Be sure your name, grade and today's date are on the Word document.*

Document 1

The word robot came from the Czech word robotta (meaning "forced labor"). Karel Capek used it in a 1921 play, "Rossum's Universal Robots". A robot is generally a mechanical apparatus doing work of a human being. A robot does not have to look human but is able to perform human actions and functions. One possible current device that could be considered a robot is the vacuum cleaner that cleans the floor without any human help. This vacuum cleaner is placed on the floor and by moving it "learns" the size and shape of the room. It then can clean the room once it is activated. Today many devices in the home, in school, and in business can be considered robots. In the future many more devices will be available to make life easier.

   A Robot

1. Where did the term robot come from?

Document 2

Asimov, a famous science fiction writer, created the three laws of robotics and they are:
1. A robot may not injure a human being or through inaction allow a human being to come to harm.
2. A robot must obey orders given it by human beings, except where such orders would conflict with the First Law.
3. A robot must protect its own existence as long as such protection does not conflict with the First or Second Law.

Because they are laws, they must be obeyed.

1. If you consider Asimov's three laws, could robots be used as soldiers in a war? Why or why not?

Document 3

In the 1939 New York World's Fair two robots, Elektro and his dog Sparko, were displayed. (see below). Elektro was 7 feet tall and looked somewhat like a human. Sparko was a robot dog that barked and waged its tail. Elektro could walk, salute, distinguish colors, say 77 words and do other tasks. Sparko, with photoelectric cells for eyes, could follow the path of a flashlight.

Illustration by Bridget Mamone

1. Do these two robots, created in 1939, resemble any robots in use today? Which ones?

Document 4

Today, robots are used extensively in manufacturing. Large robots perform complex and simple welding for many manufacturers, such as for automobiles. Robots are also used in places where it would be too difficult for a human, such as bomb disposal, or search and rescue. Robots are also used in hazardous environments such as underwater or in outer space or in volcanoes. Mobot, a 1970's robot was used to handle radioactive waste. In the future robotic planes and tanks will be used in war, saving the lives of many soldiers. Robotic devices of the future may also be used to operate on people in the hospital. In the future, robots may take the place of seeing eye dogs and help people who are visually handicapped live lives that are more productive.

1. Describe three ways that robots may be used in the future.

Document 5

Robots have had a rich history of being portrayed in movies. One of the earliest robots portrayed in the movies was the robot in the movie *Metropolis*. Another of the early "robots" could be Mary Shell's *Frankenstein* subtitled *The Modern Prometheus*. Perhaps the most famous robots to appear in movies were R2-D2 and C-3PO of *Star Wars* fame. Both came with restraining belts that keep them faithful to their human owners. Another very famous computer with human like thinking ability was HAL, in the movie *2001 A Space Odyssey*. Hal could think and when "he" felt that his existence was in jeopardy he killed his human companions. Other robots portrayed in movies include Robby, the Robocop, as well as the Terminator. Today it is possible to buy a "pet" robot that looks like a dog. The robot can perform many tricks for the human owner.

1. Do R2-D2 and C-3PO follow Asimov's three laws? Why or why not?

Document 6

Chess playing "robots" have been around for centuries. The best is IBM's Deep Blue. This robot was programmed with what appears to be human intelligence in the area of chess playing. The programs were so good that a few years ago, Deep Blue, in a series of chess games, beat the greatest chess grand master of all time in a head-to-head match. The chess grand master became so upset with how good Deep Blue was playing that he left the match in disgust. Today an even better version of Deep Blue has been used in a championship match. Today many chess playing programs that play as well as experts can be purchased for a PC. This type of program is called an expert system because it acts like an expert. The reason why the program is so good is because the expert must program his or her knowledge into the system. This means the system is only as good as the expert programming it. In the case of Deep Blue, many chess experts worked together to write the program.

1. Given the fact that a computer can now play chess better than the greatest chess player ever, is it possible that a robot can one day think? Why or why not?

Part B

For Part B, use the information from the documents, your answers in Part A, and your knowledge of robots to write a well-organized essay. In the essay you should:

> Write about the growth of robots in the 20th century and in what ways they may be superior to humans.

Students: For more information on this topic, visit the following web site and the link from this web site http://www.neuroprosthesis.org/bbook.htm.

Assessment Test 7—History of Communications

The next two assessment tests were used to explain how communications developed. The tests were used, as were all other assessment tests, as an aid to taking the assessment test and as a typing problem. I also used these two assignments as an introduction to a following topic on programming languages. As with most assessment tests, the students did not like taking them and they did not see the value in them. I had hoped that by taking my made-up exams the students would be better prepared to take the real tests but my observation was the students either did not enjoy the tests or I did not motivate them enough. Another reason could be the students wanted to rush through the exams in order to play games.

The History of Communications I

This question is based on the accompanying documents (1-5). Some of the documents have been edited for the purpose of the question. The questions are designed to test your ability to work with documents related to the history of communication. As you analyze the documents, take into account both the content of each document and any point of view that may be presented in the document.

Directions: Using the document, the answers to the questions in Part A, and your knowledge of communications, write, in Word, a well-organized essay about the history of communications. *Include your name, today's date and your grade (7th or 8th) on the first page.* You should use a font size of 14, font of Times New Roman, and margins of 1" on all four sides.

In your essay, remember to:
- Tell about the history of communications.
- Include an introduction, body, and conclusion
- Include details, examples, or reasons in developing your ideas
- Use the information from the documents in your answer to answer Part B.

Communication Background: People and animals communicate all the time. We communicate by speaking, via music, via art, by our body position and facial expressions, by visual signs such as a stop sign, and by how we dress. Early communications was necessary in order to survive. Early humans had to work and communicate together to hunt and live. Early communications consisted of forms of grunts and hand signals. After man developed physically and mentally, he began to develop an early form of speech.

Task:

For Part A, read each document carefully and answer the questions after each document. These answers will help you write your essay. Then read the directions for Part B and write your essay.

Part A
Short—Answer Questions

Directions: Read each document and answer the question or questions that follow each document by typing your answer in Word. *Be sure your name, grade and today's date are on the Word document.* Please use a font of Times New Roman and a font size of 1" on all sides.

Document 1

Early communication between humans consisted of grunts and other noises as well as hand signals and sign language. Language as we know it did not occur until much later in human development. People were able to tell what someone else wanted because simple hand signals were usually self-explanatory. Pointing or using other hand signals was usually enough for one person to understand another. This form of hand signals is still used today, one example are the directional signals you make when driving a car. An outstretched straight arm outside the window means you are making a left turn. Putting your two fingers together in the shape of a circle means every thing is OK. Many other forms of hand signals are used in different business in order for people to communicate when there is too much noise.

Modern man evolved physically to the point where he could speak by around 100,000 B.C.

 Sign Language

1. How did early humans communication with each other if they did not have a regular language?

Document 2

Illustration by Bridget Mamone

Cave drawings, such as the drawings in the Chauvet cave in France (above), often depict what early humans saw and were probably used as a means of communications and as decorations. Because these cave drawings and other pictures appear in many forms and places, it is probable that many different groups of diverse people used the same method to communicate. One form of drawings, know as pictographs appear in many different countries including America. Other forms of communications are the knotted ropes and notched sticks of the ancient Chinese, the South American Indians and the West African and Australian natives.

1. What was the purpose of early cave drawings?

Document 3

Early spoken language appears to have developed from 100,000 to 40,000 years ago. By this time, Homo Sapiens (early humans) must have been physically equipped for speech. This spoken language took the form of simple sounds that people began to understand. From these simple sounds grew a more complex form of speech. There are no documents or writings that explain where language originated. Language probably originated in several places, such as Asia and the Middle East at the same time. The oldest languages of the Asian and European family are Sanskrit, Greek and Latin in that order. Latin merged with early French, then early Spanish and then Italian. English did not develop until much later.

1. How did language originate?

Document 4

It is possible that in prehistoric times the speakers of the original Asian and European parent-language were one close group. Due to migration, people lost contact with their original homeland and clans and this allowed their speech to turn into a dialect of the original. This change in speech was the major reason for the growth of so many languages. Many languages have similar words but are a different language. An example is Italian and Spanish. Both languages have similar words but are two distinct languages.

English is very close to early German and Dutch. As a result of the Norman conquest of England, the English language acquired French and Latin words and can therefore be considered as a Germanic language with a romance language addition.

1. How did English develop?

Document 5

Writing was invented not once but perhaps as many as six separate times, in places such as China and Central America. Each attempt at formal writing began with simple pictures and plain strokes or dots. One of the earliest forms of writing began in the Fourth Millennium B.C. in Mesopotamia. The inventors of this writing were probably Sumerians and their form of writing evolved into the system of marks called cuneiform. The Sumerians used their writing for bookkeeping and for recording the texts that governed their religion. Hieroglyphic writing—a combination of pictures and signs-developed in Egypt. By the end of the Second millennium B.C. the Phoenician alphabet emerged. This alphabet is the precursor (came before) the type of text we use today.

Hieroglyphics

1. Describe two types of early writing and what they were used for.

Part B

For Part B, use the information from the documents, your answers in Part A, and your knowledge of communication to write a well-organized essay. In the essay, you should:

> Write about the early history of spoken and written communications.

This next assessment was used as a follow-up to the previous test. Some of the information is interesting but I was not sure if the information was over the students head.

Assessment Test 8—History of Communications Part II

This question is based on the accompanying documents (1-5). Some of the documents have been edited for the purpose of the question. The question is designed to test your ability to work with documents related to the history of communication. As you analyze the documents, take into account both the content of each document and any point of view that may be presented in the document.

Directions: Using the document, the answers to the questions in Part A, and your knowledge of communications write, in Word, a well-organized essay about communications. *Include your name, today's date and your grade (7th or 8th) on the first page.* Please use a font size of 14, font of Impact, margins of 1.25 on all four sides.

In your essay, remember to:
* Tell about communications as discussed in these documents.
* Include an introduction, body, and conclusion
* Include details, examples, or reasons in developing your ideas
* Use the information from the documents in your answer

Communication Background: Communication can be described as telling someone something. This can take the form of speech, writing, music, art or many other forms. Language is an expression of human activity and as activity changes language changes with it. This means as humans change their language also changes to adjust to these changes.

Task:

For Part A, read each document carefully and answer the questions after each document. These answers will help you write your essay. Then read the directions for Part B and write your essay.

Part A
Short—Answer Questions

Directions: Read each document and answer the question or questions that follow each document by typing your answer in Word. *Be sure your name, grade and today's date are on the Word document.*

Document 1

Many linguists (people who study languages) believe that the more isolated a country is, the less likely its language is to change over time, while a country that is the crossroads of many other countries, such as France will have the most change in its language over time. Many linguists also believe that war-like countries also tend to have the biggest change in its native language. This is because of the travels of its army and the interaction with other people. A language such as Sardinian, somewhat sheltered from the rest of the world, has changed very little from the original Latin, while French, exposed to invasions and as a crossroads of Europe, has changed the most.

All languages change over time. Many early settlers of America would have a hard time understanding modern English just as we would have a hard time understanding them. Both groups would find early Chaucer, a famous early English writer, impossible to understand.

1. Why would a language such as English change so much over time?

Document 2

The Romance languages are so called because they stem directly from Latin, the language of the Romans. They include French, Spanish, Portuguese, Italian and Rumanian. Some non-national languages like Provencal, Catalan and Sardinian can also be called a Romance language. This common ancestor is the reason why these languages are so similar. Although many of these languages are similar, they are still different and many words from one language cannot be understood by speakers of a different language. A good example is the spelling of words in English as used in America and English as used in England. We spell color as *color* the English spell it as *colour*. The English also have different names for things. We call a car's engine compartment a hood; the English call it a bonnet.

1. a. What is a romance language?
   b. Is Greek a romance language? Why or why not?

Document 3

Today, humans communicate by many means and via many languages. The most common language, that is the language spoken by the most people, is Chinese. This is because of the population of China. Fewer people speak English but more countries teach English than any other foreign language. English is also the language used by the airline industry. Foreign pilots who want to fly into an American airport must speak English. Many people who study these things believe that there will be a worldwide language one-day. That is, a universal language spoken by everyone. The opinion is that this language will be a form of English. One reason is the amount of travel that Americans make to other countries. In order to serve the Americans, people in other countries need to learn English. Although many people know English, few Americans know another language. English is also the dominate language spoken at the United Nations.

1. Why do more people speak Chinese than English?

Document 4

The similarities between spoken and written human language and computer languages are the same. Computer languages began as a series of numbers, which the computer could understand but only a very few good programmers were able to code. In order for a computer to understand instructions, the instructions were written in a form as close to what the computer could understand as possible. This was a series of numbers. A series of bits, or on off switches, were used to store these numbers, which were stored as the instructions for the computer. From this early beginning, computer languages, which were easier for humans to use, were developed. These languages included FORTRAN and COBOL. Other early computer languages, such as Algol were used for a short period and then were replaced by easier to use languages.

1. How were instructions stored in the computer?

Document 5

Programming languages have evolved (changed) over the years. The computer still can't understand anything other than a series of numbers but humans continue to write programs in more complex ways. These programs or instructions are converted into the language (numbers) that the computer can understand. Some modern forms of computer languages include Java which is a computer language used for web design. As computers evolve, computer languages will evolve with them to suit the needs of the industry and customers. It is expected that one-day computers will be able to be programmed by speaking in your native language to a computer, similar to what you see in science fiction movies.

Although this will happen, our speech will still need to be translated into the numbers that a computer can really understand.

1. Can a computer understand a program written in Java? Why and how, or why not?

Part B

For Part B, use the information from the documents, your answers in Part A, and your knowledge of communication to write a well-organized essay. In the essay you should:

> Write about the history of spoken language and computer languages and how computer languages are similar to human language.

Assessment Test 9—The History of Programming Languages

This assessment test was the final test used to describe how language works. The previous two tests, History of Communications Part I and II were used as a foundation so that we could discuss the topic of how humans communicate with a computer. Sometimes there is a method to what a teacher is doing!

The History of Programming Languages

This question is based on the accompanying documents (1-5). Some of the documents have been edited for the purpose of the question. The question is designed to test your ability to work with documents related to the history of programming languages. As you analyze the documents, take into account both the content of each document and any point of view that may be presented in the document.

Directions: Using the document, the answers to the questions in Part A, and your knowledge of programming languages write, in Word, a well-organized essay about programming languages. *Include your name, today's date and your grade (7th or 8th) on the first page.* Please use a font size of 14, font of Arial Black, top and bottom margins of 1.3", and side margins of 1.2".

In your essay, remember to:
- Tell about the history of programming languages as discussed in these documents.
- Include an introduction, body, and conclusion

- Include details, examples, or reasons in developing your ideas
- Use the information from the documents in your answer

Programming Language Background: Computers interact with people via languages. Computers can only understand electronic signals. These signals are sent via a stream of on off switches called bits. These signals are sent to the computer via a computer language, which we can understand and can code with. This language is then translated into a string of signals, which can be understood by the computer.

Task:

For Part A, read each document carefully and answer the questions after each document. These answers will help you write your essay. Then read the directions for Part B and write your essay.

Part A
Short—Answer Questions

Directions: Read each document and answer the question or questions that follow each document by typing your answer in Word. *Be sure your name, grade and today's date are on the Word document.*

Document 1

The way computers interact with humans is similar to the way humans interact with each other, by the use of language. Humans speak to one another and they can then understand each other. Humans communicate with computers in much the same way, via language. A computer is just a machine and at this point in time, a computer cannot understand human language to such an extent that it can perform complex functions. In order to communicate with a computer you need to communicate in a way that the computer understands. Since a computer can only understand a series of signals, which are in the form of ones and zeroes (binary language), we need to convert human language into this series of numbers in order that a computer can understand. This is performed via an intermediate program called a *compiler*. Consider a compiler as a translator. You write some instructions in some language, the compiler then converts those statements into the sequence of numbers that are finally converted into a string of on off switches that the computer can understand. The computer then carries out these instructions.

1. How does a compiler help you "talk" to a computer?

Document 2

Early computer languages were very difficult to use because they were close to the actual language of the computer. One of these early languages, still used today, is Assembler. Very few people were able to write programs because the programs were written in numbers and not words. These programmers were well paid because there were so few of them and the work they did was almost considered magic. The programs that they created, in general, were used to create reports. Both the input to the computer (the data) and the programs were on small punched cards. These cards were then "read" by a card reader and some procedure or program took place. Large printers would then print the results or reports created as the output of the program instructions. This method was used for many years, until the widespread use of PC's made entering data much easier.

1. What form was used to input the program to early computers?

Document 3

During the 1960's a small committee was created to develop a language that would be easy for humans to use. This ease of use would enable more people to be able to write programs. The committee also wanted this language to be useful to a wide spectrum of industries and the government. This language was meant to be a common language usable to many different industries. The language that was developed was called COBOL for Common Business Oriented Language. This language is the most widely used language in the world with billions of dollars spent creating and maintaining COBOL programs. An example of a simple COBOL instruction to subtract taxes from salary and place the result in a field called final-salary is: subtract taxes from salary giving final-salary. This instruction is very easy for even novice programmers to understand. Most of the programs that people were afraid would crash during the Y2K scare were written in COBOL. The Y2K scare was a real concern for many people. In the 1960's computer memory and disk storage was very limited. As a result, programmers coded a year with two digits, such as 61 for 1961. No one expected the same programs to be running 40 years later, but they were. Many companies spent many millions of dollars to have the programs rewritten with a four-digit date field in order for the programs to work on January 1, 2000. Because of the hard work and money spent, the Y2K problem did not affect many machines or programs.

1. Write a COBOL statement to: add field1 to field2 and place the result in field3.

Document 4

When the PC was first introduced, a new type of programming language was also introduced. This easy to use programming language was called BASIC. Basic is very English-like and very easy to use. This language has evolved into Visual Basic, which is much harder to use and learn but is very popular. BASIC was created because many people felt that COBOL, FORTRAN and other computer languages were too difficult for most people to learn. Visual Basic can be used to write web programs and to interface with Microsoft products, such as Access. Access is also a programming language, a database programming language. Access is also a programming language, a database programming language. Today much of the work of programming is being automated. For example, you can code a very good web site in Word without having any programming experience.

1. Is Microsoft Word a programming language? Why or why not?

Document 5

Today, computer languages are used to create systems (a group of programs) that can be used on the web. Some of the more common languages used for this purpose are Java, JavaScript, DreamWeaver, Visual Basic, C++ and HTML (Hypertext Markup Language). These languages are very popular and are used by many people to create complex systems (groups of programs). These modern programming languages will one day evolve into other programming languages just as English and other spoken languages have evolved. It is hoped that one day people will be able to talk to the computer and tell the computer what to do just by speaking in every day English or in their native language. Many computers today have very simple speech recognition programs that can understand a small number of words and instructions. As these programs improve, working with computers will become even easier. One of the reasons why speech recognition programs do not work perfectly is because of the many accents that people have. If you listen to people from different parts of the United States talk you can hardly understand them, how then can we expect a computer to understand them.

1. What might programming languages of the future look or sound like?

Part B

For Part B, use the information from the documents, your answers in Part A, and your knowledge of computer languages to write a well-organized essay. In the essay, you should:

> Write about the history of computer languages. Include information on how computer languages have changed over the years.

Students: For more information on this topic, please visit web site http://www.levenez.com/lang/.

This next assessment test was used to introduce the students to computer hardware and how computer hardware has evolved. Many students have only seen a PC and therefore can't even imagine what original computer hardware looked like.

Assessment Test 10—The History of Computer Hardware

This question is based on the accompanying documents (1-5). Some of the documents have been edited for the purpose of the question. The questions are designed to test your ability to work with documents related to the history of computer hardware. As you analyze the documents, take into account both the content of each document and any point of view that may be presented in the document.

Directions: Using the document, the answers to the questions in Part A, and your knowledge of computer hardware write, in Word, a well-organized essay about the history of computer hardware. *Include your name, today's date and your grade (7th or 8th) on the first page.* Please use a font size of 10, font of Times New Roman and default margins.

In your essay, remember to:
- Tell about the history of computer hardware as discussed in these documents.
- Include an introduction, body, and conclusion
- Include details, examples, or reasons in developing your ideas
- Use the information from the documents in your answer

Task:

For Part A, read each document carefully and answer the questions after each document. These answers will help you write your essay. Then read the directions for Part B and write your essay.

Part A
Short—Answer Questions

Directions: Read each document and answer the question or questions that follow each document by typing your answer in Word. *Be sure your name, grade and today's date are on the Word document.*

Computer Hardware History

Early computers were very large and heavy and there were only a few venders (people who sold equipment). Early computers were not programmed using written instructions but with large heavy plug boards and wire connections (see below). A "programmer" would place the wires into the holes on the board. The board was then placed into a slot into the computer. The combination of the wires into the correct slots in the board would enable the computer to perform some function. Each new program required a new set of wires and a new board.

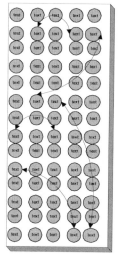

Plug board

Document 1

The following definitions can help in your understanding of computer hardware development and history.

A *mainframe* computer is a very large computer, usually located at a company's headquarters. This computer and supporting devices, such as large printers and disk drives, can often times be the size of a large room or even a house.

Mainframe tape drives

Distributed Computing is the process where by computing is done at branch offices. For example, a large bank might have its headquarters in Wall Street in downtown New York City but the bank might also have many branches throughout the New York area. Bank records are kept at the branch office and tellers at the bank offices would access the records via a terminal in the branch. This terminal is usually some form of a dumb terminal. At night, the data from the branch offices would be transmitted to the home office for update. With the advent of high speed telephone connections, this method is rarely used any more.

A "dumb" terminal is a computer with no real processing power. It consists of a monitor, keyboard and perhaps a mouse. This terminal is connected to a processor, which does the processing for the dumb terminal. These machines are very inexpensive and were widely used in many large companies. Because PC's are now so inexpensive they have generally replaced "dumb" terminals at most companies.

Centralized Computing is the process by which computing for a company is done at a large centralized site, such as a home office. The home office would create whatever reports a branch office needed and update any files needed. In this example the records would be accessed from the branch office and updated on-line.

1. What is a difference between a distributed computer system and a centralized computer system?

Document 2

There are many computer venders or makers/sellers of computer hardware. Some venders have merged with other venders, such as the current merger of HP with Compaq. Other venders have been unable to compete and are either no longer in business or make so few products as to be not relevant. A few venders, not all who are still in operation, include:

Wang
RCA
IBM
UNIVAC
Sperry UNIVAC
Honeywell
Compaq
Dell
Gateway
Apple
HP

At one time, all of these vendors made hardware and software for different types of organizations, such as banking, insurance, etc. Because of competition or other business reasons, many of these companies are no longer in business. As computer needs change and as companies invent new types of computers or new ways to use current computers, companies will evolve and they will either get larger or they will combine with other companies so that they can compete with larger companies.

1. Which of these companies have you heard of and which have you not heard of? What can you tell me about the companies you have heard about?

Document 3

Just as there are generations in human history, there are generations in computer hardware history. The first generation computers were based on circuits containing vacuum tubes and used punched cards as the storage medium. These early computers were very heavy and bulky. The next generation computers contained transistors. Transistors were invented in 1947 and they dominated the computers of the late 1950's and early 1960's. The computers that used transistors were still heavy. The third generation computers relied on the IC or Integrated Circuit. With the introduction of IC's, computers became faster and smaller.

Integrated Circuit

1. What impact did IC's have on computers?

Document 4

Fourth generation computers used microprocessors. Microprocessors located much of the computer's processing ability on a small chip. With the addition of RAM (Random Access Memory) fourth generation computers became even smaller and more powerful. The microprocessor allowed the development of personal computers (PC) that were small and cheap enough to be available to ordinary people. The first personal computer was the Altair 8800, released in 1974, but it was soon followed by the Apple I and II, the Commodore PET and eventually the IBM PC in 1981. Although processing power and storage capacity have increased with the introduction of larger IC's (Integrated Circuits), it is widely regarded that most of today's computers still belong to the fourth generation.

1. What is the difference between a third generation computer and a fourth generation computer?

Document 5

Because chips are getting smaller and more powerful, they can now be used in more places. Today's automobiles contain many chips that each performs one or more function. Most of today's cars have hundreds of tiny computer chips, each performing one or more function. Modern airplanes contain many hundreds of chips and computers. Because of the complexity of today's planes, pilots could not fly the plane without the help of the on-board computers. This type of flying is called fly-by-wire. Today's chips are getting smaller and smaller. It is expected that because of some restrictions of physics, chips may be getting close to the smallest size they can be.

An airplane consists of many on-board computers.

1. If chip size in the future is constrained (unable to go further), how will that impact computers?

Part B

For Part B, use the information from the documents, your answers in Part A, and your knowledge of computer hardware to write a well-organized essay. In the essay, you should:

> Write about the history of computer hardware.

Students: For more information on this topic, please visit web site http://accounting.rutgers.edu/raw/aies/www.bus.orst.edu/faculty/brownc/lectures/history/history.htm.

This next assessment test was used to explain how computers are being used in medicine. Computers have been used in medicine for many years and they will continue to be a big part of both diagnostic and treatment in the future. This type of assessment test is difficult to write because it contains a lot of technical information. In an attempt to make the test easier I used simple words and phrases to describe complex text.

Assessment Test 11—Computers in Medicine

This question is based on the accompanying documents (1-5). Some of the documents have been edited for the purpose of the question. The questions are designed to test your ability to work with documents related to the history of computers in medicine. As you analyze the documents, take into account both the content of each document and any point of view that may be presented in the document.

Directions: Using the document, the answers to the questions in Part A, and your knowledge of computer hardware write, in Word, a well-organized essay about the history of computers in medicine. *Include your name, today's date and your grade (7th or 8th) on the first page.* For this test, please use a font size of 12, a font of Arial, top and bottom margins of 1.2", and side margins of 1.5".

In your essay, remember to:
- Tell about the history of computers in medicine as discussed in these documents.
- Include an introduction, body, and conclusion
- Include details, examples, or reasons in developing your ideas
- Use the information from the documents in your answer

Task:

For Part A, read each document carefully and answer the questions after each document. These answers will help you write your essay. Then read the directions for Part B and write your essay.

Part A
Short—Answer Questions

Directions: Read each document and answer the question or questions that follow each document by typing your answer in Word. *Be sure your name, grade and today's date are on the Word document.*

Computers in Medicine—Early History

Computers have been used in medicine for many years. Some early uses of computers in medicine include
- Pacemaker, a device that monitors the heart
- X-ray machines
- Numerous monitoring devices

Computers are also used to maintain patient records and to perform examinations and testing and even to perform operations. Computer implants are now being used to replace defective or missing body parts. Artificial hearts, run by complex computers, will one day replace defective hearts thereby saving many lives.

Document 1

Computers have been used in medicine in one way or another for many years. About 600 years ago, the Chinese used a robot patient to train doctors in the use of acupuncture. The trainee inserted the acupuncture needles into the robot patient, a life-size bronze figure. If the needle were inserted correctly, the robot patient would squirt water out of the needle hole.

Today, computers are used to perform diagnostics (what is wrong with a patient) and treatment. Computers are used as internal devices, such as pacemakers, and to keep patients alive. Many people would not be alive today if they did not have help from a medical computer. Computers are also being used in more complex ways, such as mechanical arms and legs and ears, and computers are also being used to operate on patients. One day an artificial heart, run by complex computers, will replace defective hearts thereby saving many lives.

1. Describe two ways that computers are being used in medicine.

Document 2

Software programs have been and are currently being used in medicine in many ways.

Some early medical computer programs include:
MYCIN—1976, this program gave advice on diagnosis and therapy for infectious diseases.
Doctor, 1970's, this program interacted with a "patient". The patient was someone entering questions and receiving answers at a terminal. The program acted like a psychiatrist and worked to solve a person's problem. This program was so popular on college campuses that students would logon all night and talk with the "psychiatrist".

Other medical software includes software that helps in creating new medicines, and software that helped decode the human genetic code. Software is being used to store vast amounts of medical history in order for doctors to better analyze a persons symptoms. In the future, software will be used to analyze a person's blood and tell what is wrong with them. Software is used to run much of the equipment in hospitals and doctor offices. Software is also used to run implanted devices, such as pacemakers and artificial limbs and ears.

1. Describe two software products that are currently used in medicine.

Document 3

A surgeon in a hospital might use a computer 85% of the time, and may use up to fifty different computers in a single day. The computers make diagnosis and therapy more accurate because they have a great deal of information immediately available in the computer, not only about a patient but about the disease or problem, the patient may be having. Surgeons use computers to keep patients alive during operations (heart operations). Surgeons also use computers to monitor all aspects of a patient's health before, during, and after an operation. Computers are also used to monitor medicine that a patient receives. Some hospital devices allow a patient to distribute medicine to themselves. The machine will register the medicine and will not allow the patient to overdose.

1. Surgeons use computers for medical reasons. Describe two ways that surgeons use computers.

Document 4

Computers and communications play a big role in medicine. One simple, yet important device is the beeper. Doctors use the beeper to keep in touch with their office and with the hospitals where they work. Another device important to doctors is the cell phone. Doctors who are on call (available for patient or hospital assistance) can be reached anywhere.

Computer devices are being implanted into patients every day. An example of an implanted device is the device used to help people who are deaf to hear. This device is implanted in a person's ear and along with an external receiver a deaf person can now enjoy being able to hear.

Artificial arms and legs are now being developed that will enable amputees to use their artificial limbs almost like a real arm or leg. The computers in the prosthesis will simulate movement but not feeling. Prosthesis devices will one day look and act almost as well as real human parts.

1. Give two examples of how computers are being used today in medicine.

Document 5

Today, hospitals could not exist without computers. Computers are used in hospitals for record keeping, such as patient history and treatment history. Keeping accurate records not only protects the patients but the doctors and hospital as well. Computers are also used to monitor the vital signs of the patients and to administer the correct dosage of medicine.

In the future computer robots will be used to perform accurate operations with limited manual intervention. These robots are currently being used experimentally in several hospitals. These robots can also be used remotely, that is, the surgeon does not have to be in the same room or even in the same hospital as the robot. Using TV monitors the surgeon will be able to operate even if s(he) is in a different city from the patient. This can be a great benefit for those hospitals that do not have a particular specialist available.

1. Would treatment by robots be safer than operations by human doctors? Explain your answer.

Part B

For Part B, use the information from the documents, your answers in Part A, and your knowledge of computer hardware to write a well-organized essay. In the essay, you should:

> Write about the history of computers in medicine.

This assessment was given to show the students how computer games have evolved. Computer games have been around almost from the beginning of computer development and continue to be an important use of computers today. Think about how often you play solitaire at work. The questions were rather easy and I think the students enjoyed this test.

Assessment Test 12—The History of Computer Games

This question is based on the accompanying documents (1-5). Some of the documents have been edited for the purpose of the question. The questions are designed to test your ability to work with documents related to the history of computer games. As you analyze the documents, take into account both the content of each document and any point of view that may be presented in the document.

Directions: Using the document, the answers to the questions in Part A, and your knowledge of computer games write, in Word, a well-organized essay about the history of computer games. *Include your name, today's date and your grade (7th or 8th) on the first page.* Please use a font size of 14, font of Bookman Old Style, and all four margins of 1.25".

In your essay, remember to:
- Tell about the history of computer games as discussed in these documents.
- Include an introduction, body, and conclusion

- Include details, examples, or reasons in developing your ideas
- Use the information from the documents in your answer

Task:

For Part A, read each document carefully and answer the questions after each document. These answers will help you write your essay. Then read the directions for Part B and write your essay.

Part A
Short—Answer Questions

Directions: Read each document and answer the question or questions that follow each document by typing your answer in Word. *Be sure your name, grade and today's date are on the Word document.*

Computer Game History

Computer games have been around since the early days of computers. Computer games vary in use today from solitaire to complex Simms's and chess playing software. Complex computer simulators allow people to learn new skills, such as flying a plane to learning how to operate. Other computer games include software such as Zelda and Dungeons and Dragons. Computer games come in all sizes and run on all types of devices from computers to PlayStations to the XBox. These games and many others allow a person to interact with a machine and in some cases to learn some new skill while they are having fun.

Document 1

Computer games have been around since the early days of computers. One of the first and most famous computer games was Arthur Samuel's checker playing program. Samuel worked from 1947 to 1967 building this game. This game was a result of a research project that was designed to see if a program could learn from experience; that is, could the program learn from its mistakes. In 1968, Donald Waterman developed a computer program that learns to play draw poker. This program included an estimation of an opponent's ability to bluff. One of the earliest computers games was a version of Tic-Tac-Toe. Tic-Tac-Toe is very easy to program and creating a version of this games is often used as an assignment in a college programming course.

Another early computer game was SpaceWar. This was one of the first games specifically written to run on a computer. SpaceWar was a two-player game involving warring spaceships firing photon torpedoes. Each player could maneuver a spaceship and score by firing missiles at his opponent while trying to avoid the gravitational pull of the sun.

Several other early games include Missile Command, Centipede, Battlezone and Tempest. These games and others started as arcade games that were rewritten to run on a home computer or an Atari game machine. Another early computer game, although it ran on your TV screen, was Pong. This simple game involved a ball slowly bouncing off various walls on the screen.

1. Describe two early computer games.

Document 2

In 1977, Pac-Man was introduced. This game came with a controller and you used your TV as the screen. A controller is like a joystick (see below). The game was so popular that it was followed with a female version. The company that created Pac-Man, Atari, sold 10 million copies of the game and made a profit of 150 million dollars from just that one game. Other computer games, which usually were initially arcade games, were soon introduced. Arcade games could be found at movie theaters and amusement parks. When computers became smaller and more powerful, computer games also became more powerful. Powerful speakers and better controllers enable a person to play better and to enjoy the experience better. Computer games can now be found as an extra on movie DVD's and as accessories with cell phones.

 Controller

o   What computer games do you use and what computer device does the game play on?

Document 3

Computer games have evolved into simulation programs. Some of these simulation programs have been used to train pilots, doctors, soldiers and others. A simulator attempts to give the user a real world experience. Simulators are used today in driver's education classes. Simulators are also used in real estate to enable a person to "walk" through a house that is for sale. Simulators work very much like a computer game in the way that they interact with a user. Some types of simulators involve the use of a helmet with special glasses and perhaps special gloves. This type of a simulator is usually called virtual reality. Although simulators are not perfect, in the future with more memory and storage, a simulator will be as close to a real world experience as possible.

1. Explain two ways that simulators are being used today.

Document 4

People have often felt that one day a computer would be the greatest chess player in the world. In the late 1990's the IBM chess program, Deep Blue beat the greatest human chess player of all time in a head to head match. Today, an even better chess playing computer program is playing against the same human chess champion. Some games, such as GO, may never be able to be played well on a computer because of the complex rules of the game. Many types of board and card games are available for a modern computer.

 Game of Go

1. If a chess program can beat a human, does the chess program think? Why or why not?

Document 5

Today, entire racks of computer games can be found in any electronic store. The games are as simple as solitaire to as complex as Sims's and chess playing programs. Other computer games include the Gameboys and Xbox machines. These are hand held or small desktop devices that allow one or more people to play complex games. Computer games are now a feature of cell phones. You can now play a game on your phone without the need of any special software or computer. Computer games can now be played on-line with people that you have never met.

Part B

For Part B, use the information from the documents, your answers in Part A, and your knowledge of computer hardware to write a well-organized essay. In the essay, you should:

Write about the history of computer games.

This assessment test was used to give the students more practice on taking the test and to give them some knowledge about how the mail is delivered. The test was also used to show how technology could change a simple process such as delivering the mail. This exercise also gave them more experience on typing and composing sentences and paragraphs. I used funny clip art to make the test more enjoyable.

Assessment Test 13—The Postal Service

This question is based on the accompanying documents (1-5). Some of the documents have been edited for the purpose of the question. The questions are designed to test your ability to work with documents related to the history of the postal service. As you analyze the documents, take into account both the content of each document and any point of view that may be presented in the document.

Directions: Using the document, the answers to the questions in Part A, and your knowledge of the postal service write, in Word, a well-organized essay about the history of the postal service. Include your name, today's date and your grade (7th or 8th) on the first page. Please use a font size of 12, font of Times New Roman, and all four margins of 1.25".

In your essay, remember to:
Tell about the history of the postal service as discussed in these documents.
Include an introduction, body, and conclusion
Include details, examples, or reasons in developing your ideas
Use the information from the documents in your answer

Task:

For Part A, read each document carefully and answer the questions after each document. These answers will help you write your essay. Then read the directions for Part B and write your essay.

Part A

Short—Answer Questions

Directions: Read each document and answer the question or questions that follow each document by typing your answer in Word. Be sure your name, grade and today's date are on the Word document.

The Postal Service

The Postal Service started while the United States was still a confederation of colonies. Benjamin Franklin was named the first Postmaster General in 1775. The postal system that Congress created helped bind the new nation together, support the flow of commerce, and ensure a free flow of ideas and information. During its history, the postal service has seen many technological changes, each of which helped the mail get delivered faster and more reliably.

Document 1

In early colonial times, correspondents depended on friends, merchants, and Native Americans to carry messages between the colonies. The Postal Service started while the United States was still a confederation of colonies. Benjamin Franklin was named the first Postmaster General in 1775. The postal system that Congress created helped bind the new nation together, support the flow of commerce, and ensure a free flow of ideas and information. Local authorities operated post routes within the colonies. Then, in 1673, Governor Francis Lovelace of New York set up a monthly post between New York and Boston. The service was of short duration, but the post rider's trail became known as the Old Boston Post Road, part of today's U.S. Route 1. William Penn established Pennsylvania's first post office in 1683. In the South, private messengers, usually slaves connected the huge plantations; a hog's head of tobacco was the penalty for failing to relay mail to the next plantation.

In 1730, Alexander Spotswood, a former lieutenant governor of Virginia, became Deputy Postmaster General for America. His most notable achievement probably was the appointment of Benjamin Franklin as postmaster of Philadelphia in 1737. Franklin was only 31 years old at the time, the struggling printer and publisher of The Pennsylvania Gazette. Later he would become one of the most popular men of his age.

In 1760, Franklin reported a surplus to the British Postmaster General, a first for the postal service in North America. When Franklin left office, post roads operated from Maine to Florida and from New York to Canada, and mail between the colonies and the motor country operated on a regular schedule, with posted times.

1. In the early days of the United States, how was mail delivered?

Document 2

Central postal organization came to the colonies only after 1691 when Thomas Neale received a 21-year grant from the British Crown for a North American postal service. Neale never visited America. Instead, he appointed Governor Andrew Hamilton of New Jersey as his Deputy Postmaster General. Neale's franchise cost him only 80 cents a year but was no bargain; he died heavily in debt, in 1699, after assigning his interests in America to Andrew Hamilton.

In the early part of the 19th century, envelopes were not used. Instead, a letter was folded and the address placed on the outside of the sheet. The customer had to take a letter to the post office to mail it, and the addressee had to pick up the letter at the post office, unless he or she lived in one of about forty big cities where a carrier would deliver it to the home address for an extra penny or two.

Although postage stamps became available in 1847, mailers had the option of sending their letters and having the recipients pay the postage until 1855, when prepayment became necessary.

1. How was mail delivered in the early 19th century?

Document 3

In the first half of the 19th century, the population of the Unites States began to flow steadily into the newly acquired territories of Louisiana, Oregon and California. When gold was discovered in California in 1848, the pioneer movement quickened, and a faster way was needed to carry mail to California because mail from one coast to the other often took months.

In March 1860, an advertisement in newspapers read as follows; "Wanted: Young, skinny, wiry fellows not over 18. Must be expert riders willing to risk death daily. Orphans preferred." This was the start of the Pony Express, a new way to deliver mail. Starting in April 3, 1860, the Pony Express ran through parts of Missouri,

Kansas, Nebraska, Colorado, Wyoming, Utah, Nevada, and California. On an average day, a rider covered 75 to 100 miles. From April 1860 through June 1861, the Pony Express operated as a private enterprise. From July 1, 1861, it operated under contract as a mail route until October 24, 1861, when the transcontinental telegraph line was completed, and the Pony Express became a legend.

Pony Express

1. How did technology cause the demise (end) of the Pony Express?

Document 4

Throughout its history, the Postal Service has explored faster, more efficient forms of mail transportation. Technologies now commonplace; railroads, automobiles, and airplanes; were embraced by the Post Office Department when they were new and unworkable by many.

One such technology remains only a footnote in the history of mail delivery. On June 8, 1959, in a move a postal official heralded as "of historic significance to the peoples of the entire world," the Navy submarine U.S.S. Barbero fired a guided missile carrying 3,000 letters at the Naval Auxiliary Air Station in Mayport, Florida. "Before man reaches the moon," the official was quoted as saying, "mail will be delivered within hours from New York to California, to Britain, to India or Australia by guided missiles."

History proved differently, but this experiment with missile mail exemplifies the pioneering spirit of the Post Office Department when it came to developing faster, better ways of moving the mail.

Missile Mail

1. Why do you think missile mail failed?

Document 5

The United States government had been slow to recognize the potential of the airplane. The Post Office Department, however, was intrigued with the possibility of carrying mail by airplane and authorized its first experimental mail flight in 1911. Later, in 1911 and 1912, the Department authorized 52 experimental flights at fairs, carnivals, and air meets in more than 25 states. These flights convinced the Department that the airplane could carry a payload of mail, and officials repeatedly urged Congress after 1912 to appropriate money to launch airmail service. Congress finally authorized use of $50,000 for airmail experiments in 1916. On May 15, 1918, the Post Office Department began scheduled airmail service between New York and Washington, D.C. Simultaneous takeoffs were made from Washington's Polo Grounds and from Belmont Park, Long Island, both trips by way of Philadelphia.

These early mail planes had no instruments, radios, or other navigational aids. Pilots flew by dead reckoning or "by the seat of their pants." Forced landings occurred frequently because of bad weather, but fatalities in those early months were rare, largely because of the small size, maneuverability, and slow landing speed of the planes.

Congress authorized airmail postage of 24 cents, including special delivery. The public was reluctant to use this more expensive service, and, during the first year, airmail bags contained as much regular mail as airmail.

1. Explain how airmail service developed in the United States.

Part B

For Part B, use the information from the documents, your answers in Part A, and your knowledge of the postal service to write a well-organized essay. In the essay, you should:

> Write about the history of the postal service. Include information on how technology changed the way mail was delivered.

Students: If you would like more information on this topic, please visit Web site: http://www.usps.com/history/history/his1.htm.

This next assessment test was used to give the students more practice on taking the test and to give them some knowledge about the history of the telephone. The test was also used to show how technology could change so fast and so dramatically. Not only has the telephone changed, but also computers have changed rapidly and that change has affected every aspect of our lives.

Assessment Test 14—The Telephone

This question is based on the accompanying documents (1-5). Some of the documents have been edited for the purpose of the question. The questions are designed to test your ability to work with documents related to the history of the telephone. As you analyze the documents, take into account both the content of each document and any point of view that may be presented in the document.

Directions: Using the document, the answers to the questions in Part A, and your knowledge of the telephone write, in Word, a well-organized essay about the history of the postal service. Include your name, today's date and your grade (7th or 8th) on the first page. Please use a font size of 13, font of Times New Roman, and all four margins of 1".

In your essay, remember to:
Tell about the history of the telephone and telephone service as discussed in these documents.
Include an introduction, body, and conclusion
Include details, examples, or reasons in developing your ideas
Use the information from the documents in your answer

Task:

For Part A, read each document carefully and answer the questions after each document. These answers will help you write your essay. Then read the directions for Part B and write your essay.

Part A
Short—Answer Questions

Directions: Read each document and answer the question or questions that follow each document by typing your answer in Word. Be sure your name, grade and today's date are on the Word document.

The Telephone

Americans talk over the telephone more than any other people do. Next to the Bible, phone directories are read more than any other publication. The telephone was developed by many different people from many counties. The telephone has been an important part of our lives for many years. The advanced technology of communications aided by transistorized electronics and computers has made the telephone a versatile instrument. As the telephone developed, society changed with it. From a simple hand crank machine to tiny cell phones, telephones have evolved to the point where just about everyone has a phone in their pocket or purse.

Document 1

The telephone was not invented by one person but rather was developed by building on the work of others. Alexander Graham Bell, a young Scottish speech teacher, untutored in electricity, is created with inventing the telephone in 1876. The English scientist Robert Hooke made the first suggestions on how speech might be transmitted over long distances. In 1796, the German scientist G. Huth suggested that acoustical telephony might be tried. He had the idea that during clear nights mouth trumpets or speaking tubes could be used to pass a shouted message from one tower to another. Huth named this speaking tube the telephone. Other people whose experiments contributed to the invention of the telephone were Charles Grafton Page who discovered in 1837 that when there are rapid changes in the magnetism of iron, it gives off a musical note. Philip Reis of Germany became the first to transmit a musical melody electrically over a distance.

1. Many people are credited with the invention of the telephone. Discuss three people who contributed to the development of the telephone and what their contribution was.

Document 2

Two Americans were working on telephonic transmission in 1875, independently of and unknown to each other. One was Elisha Gray; the other was Alexander Graham Bell. Gray filed his patent on February 14, 1876. On the same day, but only a few hours earlier, Bell had applied for a patent for the same type of instrument. In later years, there was a great deal of bitter legal dispute about the patent, but in the end, Bell was awarded the patent rights and he received the credit for his invention. Over 600 lawsuits were filed to challenge Bell's patent but in the end, his patent was allowed.

On March 10, 1876 Bell spoke the first complete sentence on his invention, "Mr. Watson, come here, I want you." Although these early calling devices were crude and communications were poor, development was rapid in the United States. Bell wanted to sell his invention to Western Union for $100,000 but Western Union was so sure of its own service (the telegraph) and also sure that the telephone would never work for long distances that it refused to purchase the invention. As a result Bell continued to refine his invention and to form a new company called the Bell Telephone Company.

1. Why is Alexander Graham Bell given credit for inventing the telephone?
2. What is a patent?

Document 3

In the early days of the telephone system, a wire connection was needed for each person that you wanted to speak to. As the phone system grew this physical constraint meant that you required a large number of wires for each phone. Switchboards and many telephone operators removed this requirement but this also meant the phone company needed to hire many people to switch calls via a switchboard.

During the birth of the phone company many discoveries were made that helped not only the development of the phone system but computers as well. Some of these non-technical advances included the following.
On January 28, 1878, the first commercial switchboard began operating in New Haven Connecticut.
On February 21, 1878 the world's first telephone directory came out.
In 1878 the Rutherford B. Hayes administration installed the first telephone in the White House.
On February 28, 1885 AT&T was formed. AT&T handled long distance calls for the phone company.
In 1889 the first public coin telephone came into use in Hartford Connecticut. The first pay phones were attended, with payment going to someone standing nearby.

Switchboard

1. Describe three advances to the original phone system.

Document 4

Additional advances occurred in the 20th century that helped the phone system evolve but also contributed to the birth of other technical devices such as the computer. In the early 20th century two devices, the triode and vacuum tubes would be used and make possible radiotelephony, microwave transmission, radar, television, and hundreds of other technologies. Telephone repeaters could now span the country enabling a nationwide telephone system. As evidence of the triode's success, on January 25, 1915 the first transcontinental telephone line opened between New York City and San Francisco. In 1921 the Bell System introduced the first commercial panel switch. It offered many innovations and many problems. Although customers could dial out themselves, the number of parts and its operating method made it noisy for callers. Working like a game of Snakes and Ladders, the switch used selectors to connect calls, with the arms moving up and down in large banks of contacts.

In 1927, commercial long distance radio-telephone service was introduced between the United States and Great Britain. They expanded it later to communicate with Canada, Australia, South Africa, Egypt and Kenya as well as ships at sea.

1. Explain two advances to the phone system in the early 20th century.

Document 5

Cell phones are a recent invention that has grown to the point where just about everyone either has or will have a phone in their pocket or purse. In the future people will be able to use their phones as a mini computer, retrieve e-mail, and surf the net while walking on the street. Cell phones will probably not get smaller but instead will get bigger in order for the phone to have more features. Extra features that one day will probably be attached to a cell phone include, the ability to play games over the internet, the ability to use the cell phone as a writing instrument, the ability to use the cell phone as a musical device, as well as many other features that can only be dreamed about. With the growth of cell phones it is very possible that home phones, phones that are attached to wires in the walls, will one day soon no longer be necessary.

1. What might the cell phone be used for in the future?

Part B

For Part B, use the information from the documents, your answers in Part A, and your knowledge of the telephone and telephone service to write a well-organized essay. In the essay, you should:

> Write about the history of the telephone. Include information on how technology changed through the years.

Students: If you would like additional information on this topic, please visit Web site: http://www.privateline.com/TelephoneHistoryA/TeleHistoryA.htm.

This next assessment test was used to give the students more practice on taking the test and to give them some knowledge about the history of animation and special effects and how computers became a big part of that advance. The test was also used to show how animation and special effect technology has changed through the years. Young children are intrigued with this topic and I felt it would be easy to explain how computers assist in making the special effects that they see on the screen.

Assessment Test 15—Animation and Movie Special Effects

This question is based on the accompanying documents (1-5). Some of the documents have been edited for the purpose of the question. The questions are designed to test your ability to work with documents related to the history of the animation and special effects. As you analyze the documents, take into account both the content of each document and any point of view that may be presented in the document.

Directions: Using the document, the answers to the questions in Part A, and your knowledge of the telephone write, in Word, a well-organized essay about the history of the animation and special effects. Be sure to include any information present that shows how computers help create the special effects. Include your name, today's date and your grade (7th or 8th) on the first page. Please use a font size of 13, font of Times New Roman, and all four margins of 1".

In your essay, remember to:
Tell about the history of animation and special effects as discussed in these documents.
Include an introduction, body, and conclusion
Include details, examples, or reasons in developing your ideas

Use the information from the documents in your answer

Task:

For Part A, read each document carefully and answer the questions after each document. These answers will help you write your essay. Then read the directions for Part B and write your essay.

Part A
Short—Answer Questions

Directions: Read each document and answer the question or questions that follow each document by typing your answer in Word. Be sure your name, grade and today's date are on the Word document.

Animation and Special Effects

Since the beginnings of time, human beings have tried to capture a sense of motion in their art. This sense of trying to capture motion has led humans to create cartoons and now to creating movies with many special effects. The modern process of creating these special effects would not be possible without computers.

Document 1

Since the beginnings of time, human beings have tried to capture a sense of motion in their art. From the cave painting of an eight-legged boar in Northern Spain, which tried to simulate motion, to paintings alongside the remains of long-dead pharaohs, this quest for capturing motion has been a common theme throughout many of mankind's artistic endeavors.

Special effects in movies can be traced back to the late nineteenth century and the father of special effects, Georges Méliès. He created special effects in early silent films by the use of stop action filming and marionettes. By stopping the film, then restarting the film he could make objects appear and disappear as if by magic. Most of the special effects used today can be traced back to him.

A relatively easy special effect uses the effects of perspectives. It is a standard trick of perspective that two objects exactly the same size can be made to appear smaller and larger in relation to each other. For example, if you have two tennis balls, hold one close to your face and the other at arms length, and then look at the two balls with one eye closed, the two balls will seem to be of different sizes. The one closer to your face will appear much larger than the other will. This principle has been used to film many scenes starting with the films of Méliès.

Cave Painting

1. What is a perspective?

Document 2

Many people believe that the history of special effects in the movies begins with the movie *2001: A Space Odyssey* (1968). Until the Star Wars era began in the late 1970's, *2001: A Space Odyssey* was the best-known science fiction film ever made. The real achievement of 2001 was its use of special visual effects to create an experience in the theater. Other popular films were made that used special effects to create "disaster" movies. Two of the most popular were *The Poseidon Adventure* and *Earthquake*. With the movie *Earthquake*, special effects and sound effects gave the audience the feeling of being in an earthquake. Sound effects expanded with the addition of digital technology. In the movie *Jurassic Park*, when the dinosaur ran or hit the ground, you could almost feel the movie theatre shake. In the 1950's and 1960's a new form of special effects, 3D, was added to movies. Watching a 3D movie required the viewer to wear a special pair of glasses. Although 3D movies never became very popular, sometimes a 3D movie will be made as a special feature. A very popular 3D attraction in Disney World, one that is no longer in the theme park, was the movie *Captain EO*. Because of the high level of 3D used to make this movie, the movie was very realistic. A new 3D movie, called *Honey I Shrunk The Audience*, is now showing in Disney World.

1. How did the introduction of digital sound enhance the viewer's movie experience?

Document 3

Special effects in the 1980's and 1990 have advanced because of the growth of computer power and special camera techniques. Many of the movies of this period still used the stop and go technique first used by Méliès. Some examples include, *The Empire Strikes Back*, *Dragonslayer*, *E.T. the Extra-Terrestrial* and others. *Tron*, a movie that takes place in a computer, inspired many people to enter the field of computer graphics. The movie, *Young Sherlock Holmes* used a combination of live-action, computer graphics, and stop motion to create eye-opening effects. In this movie, the knight from the stain glass window was the first fully computer animated character in a full-length film. The Oscar winning movie, *Who Framed Roger Rabbit*, incorporated live action with traditional cell animation. For the movie *The Abyss*, the computer graphics team worked for eight months to create 75 seconds of screen time.

1. Describe three movie special effects from movies.

Document 4

Special effects in movies have advanced to the point where dinosaurs interact with humans (*Jurassic Park*) and tens of thousands of clones have a major battle on some far away planet (*Star Wars II*). Although the special effects in *Jurassic Park* were not perfect, many of the scenes were so good that people could almost believe that dinosaurs were alive again. In the movie *Spiderman,* you could imagine a person using a web to fly. The software that is used to create these special effects is complex and the effects generated can take months to create. In most cases special computers, special software and specially trained programmers are needed to create these effects. Because of the complexity of creating these special effects, it often takes longer to create the effects than it takes to create the rest of the movie. As many as 100 individual artists and animators worked more than 2.5 million computer hours to create the movie version of "The Hulk".

1. Why does it take so long to create special effects for the movies?

Document 5

Today computer animation is used in almost all movies. It is expected that one day computers will be so powerful and software so good that actors will no longer be necessary, they will all be computer generated. A recent movie used just such a situation as its plot.

Today, the motion picture is our most powerful and expressive storytelling medium. Much of its impact lies in the fact that it is a photographic medium. To many people, "seeing is believing." Special effects make it easier for people to believe.

1. Would a computer-generated movie with no movie actors be a good idea? Why?

Part B

For Part B, use the information from the documents, your answers in Part A, and your knowledge of animation and special effects to write a well-organized essay. In the essay, you should:

> Write about the history of animation and special effects. Be sure to include any information regarding the use of computers in creating the special effects.

Students: If you would like additional information on this topic, please visit Web site: http://www-viz.tamu.edu/courses/viza615/97spring/history.html.

This assessment test was used to give the students information regarding a recent topic that they were learning in their history/social studies class. Some of the information was advanced but all of the information is interesting.

Assessment Exam 16—The Civil War

This question is based on the accompanying documents (1-5). Some of the documents have been edited for the purpose of the question. The question is designed to test your ability to work with documents related to the Civil War. As you analyze the documents, take into account both the content of each document and any point of view that may be presented in the document.

Directions: Using the document, the answers to the questions in Part A, and your knowledge of the Civil War, write, in Word, a well-organized essay about the role of the Civil War in the history of our country. You should use a font of 14, font type of Times New Roman, margins of 1.25" for top and bottom, and 1" on both sides.

In your essay, remember to:
- Tell about people and events of the Civil War, the impact the war had on both sides, and the impact the war had on America.
- Include an introduction, body, and conclusion
- Include details, examples, or reasons in developing your ideas
- Use the information from the documents in your answer

Civil War Background:

The Civil War was one of the defining events in American History. More people died in battle in this war, 600,000 to 650,000 or 2% of the population, than in any other war America has fought. This is such an important event in American history that fifty thousand (50,000) books have already been published about the war with dozens of new books published each year.

Task:

For Part A, read each document carefully and answer the questions after each document. These answers will help you write your essay. Then read the directions for Part B and write your essay.

Part A
Short—Answer Questions

Directions: Read each document and answer the question or questions that follow each document by typing your answer in Word. *Be sure your name, grade and today's date are on the Word document.*

Document 1

Fort Sumter was attacked on April 12, 1861. Most people define this event as the start of the Civil War but rumblings that lead to the Civil War had been going on for some time. In some ways the war was about the slaves; the South needed the slaves for their farms and the North, because of their strong manufacturing capabilities, did not need slaves and felt that slavery was wrong. The war was also about states right; the rights of states to make decisions without interference from the Federal government.

The first major battle of the war was Bull Run or as the South called the battle, First Manassas. During the war a second battle was fought in the same place and was also called Bull Run or Second Manassas. This first battle took place on Wilmer McLean's farm. McLean became so nervous about this battle that he left his farm and moved south and west to near Appomattox Court House. This was the location of the last major battle of the Civil War and is where General Lee surrendered his army of the South to General Grant. Therefore the first and last major battle of the war took place on Wilmer McLean's property.

The war was so large and effected so much of America because it took place in so many places; 10,000 different places from New Mexico to Tennessee to Vermont to the Florida coast.

1. What was a major cause of the Civil War? Explain.

Document 2

Fredrick Douglass was an ex-slave who was a strong voice of anti-slavery and a powerful orator. Fredrick Douglass was born a slave on Maryland's eastern shore in 1818. At age eight he went to live with his master's son-in-law in Baltimore, where he was treated well. He stayed on for a dozen years and taught himself to read and write. In September of 1838, dressed as a sailor, he boarded a train and headed north and to freedom. He soon found himself in New Bedford Mass, whose abolitionist population made it a safe haven. In the propaganda war against slavery, Douglass's speeches and his best-selling autobiography, *Narrative of the Life of Fredrick Douglass*, were powerful tools against slavery. He moved to Rochester, New York and started a newspaper, the *North Star*. As a Republican he craved public office; however he never received other than low level appointments such as Marshall of the District of Columbia. He died in 1895.

1. How did Fredrick Douglas help in the fight against slavery?

Document 3

Uncle Tom's Cabin or *Life Among the Lowly* was written in 1852 by Harriet Beecher Stowe. The novel is believed to have had a profound effect on the North's view of slavery. The novel depicts the harsh reality of slavery while also showing that Christian love and faith can overcome even something as evil as slavery. Uncle Tom's Cabin was the best selling novel of the century after the Bible and is created with helping to fuel the abolitionist cause in the 1850's. More than 300,000 books were sold in the United States within the year and a million and a half pirated copies were in print world wide. Prior to the Civil War, Harriet Beecher Stowe and her husband made their home in Cincinnati, Ohio, just across the Ohio River from Kentucky, a slave state. She only made brief visits to Kentucky towns and was never on a slave plantation. Most of the book was written in Brunswick Maine.

1. Piracy or the illegal copying of something has been going on for centuries. Contrast the difference, if any, of the pirating of a game CD today and the book *Uncle Tom's Cabin*.

Document 4

General Robert E. Lee was a career U.S. Army officer and the most celebrated general of the Confederate forces during the American Civil War. He entered the United States Military Academy in 1825. When he graduated in 1829, second in his class of 46, not only had he attained the top academic record, but he had no demerits. A demerit is given for bad behavior. After the war, as a college professor, Lee supported President Andrew Johnson's program of Reconstruction and intersectional friendship between the North and the South. He urged reconciliation between the North and South, and allowing former Confederates into the Nation's political life. Lee became the great Southern hero of the war, and his popularity grew in the North as well as the South.

Ulysses S. Grant was an American general and politician who was elected the 18th President of the United States. At the age of 17, he barely passed the United States Military Academy's height requirement for entrance. He graduated from West Point in 1843, ranking 21st in a class of 39. He achieved international fame as the leading Union general in the American Civil War. He has been described as the greatest general of his age and one of the greatest strategists of any age. His Vicksburg Campaign has been reviewed by military specialists around the world. Grant announced generous terms for his defeated foes, and pursued a policy of peace.

1. What are two similarities between Generals Lee and Grant?

Document 5

America has a long sea coast, stretching from Maine to Florida. In addition, America has many long rivers that run through the heart of the country, such as the Mississippi. Because of this it was inevitable that sea battles would be fought during the Civil War. At the start of the war all ships on both sides were made of wood but both sides knew that ships made of metal would have the advantage over wooden ships. The South refitted a Northern wooden ship called the *Virginia* and rechristened this new iron clad ship the *Merrimack*. The North meanwhile had built a new iron clad called the *USS Monitor*. The *Monitor* was a new type of ship that contained 47 patented devices. All of the *Monitor's* features except the turret and pilothouse were underwater, making it the first semi-submersible ship. In contrast, the *Merrimack* was a conventional wooden vessel covered with iron plates. On March 8, 1862 the *Merrimack* attached the Union ships blockading Hampton Roads, Virginia. During this battle the *Merrimack* destroyed the Union ships the *Cumberland* and the *Congress* and nearly destroyed the ship *Minnesota*. The next day the *Monitor* arrived and fought the *Merrimack* to a draw. This was the first battle of iron clad ships and after that battle no new ships were made of wood.

1. What are any benefits to iron clad ships?

Part B

For Part B, use the information from the documents, your answers in Part A, and your knowledge of the Civil War to write a well-organized essay. In the essay, you should:

> Write about the history of the Civil War including causes and effect.

This next assessment included a discussion on the solar system. I gave this test after I noticed that the students were learning about the planets. I updated the exam with the information regarding the change in Pluto's status.

Assessment Exam 17—Our Solar System

This question is based on the accompanying documents (1-5). Some of the documents have been edited for the purpose of the question. The question is designed to test your ability to work with documents related to our solar system. As you analyze the documents, take into account both the content of each document and any point of view that may be presented in the document.

Directions: Using the document, the answers to the questions in Part A, and your knowledge of our solar system, write, in Word, a well-organized essay about our solar system. You should use a font of 14, font type of Times New Roman, margins of 1.25" for top and bottom, and 1" on both sides.

In your essay, remember to:
- Tell about our solar system, the planets, and other bodies in the solar system.
- Include an introduction, body, and conclusion
- Include details, examples, or reasons in developing your ideas
- Use the information from the documents in your answer

Solar System Background:

Our solar system currently consists of nine planets, the sun, and other smaller objects, such as asteroids. Pluto has recently been renamed as a dwarf planet. This change occurred because numerous other objects larger than Pluto had been found and if Pluto remained a planet the other objects would have been classified as planets. These objects as well as Pluto are now called dwarf planets.

Task:

For Part A, read each document carefully and answer the questions after each document. These answers will help you write your essay. Then read the directions for Part B and write your essay.

Part A
Short—Answer Questions

Directions: Read each document and answer the question or questions that follow each document by typing your answer in Word. *Be sure your name, grade and today's date are on the Word document.*

Document 1

The solar system had nine planets. These planets, starting from their nearness to the Sun, are: Mercury, Venus, Earth, Mars, Jupiter, Saturn Neptune, Uranus and Pluto. When you rank the planets by size, from smallest to largest the order becomes: Pluto, Mercury, Mars, Venus, Earth, Uranus, Neptune, Saturn and Jupiter. Astronomers are debating whether Pluto is a planet and if other objects recently found are planets. Based on this discussion and the possible new definition of a planet it is possible that many million years from now our moon would be a classified as a planet. As a result of this discussion Pluto has now been reclassified as a dwarf planet. Several other objects that were recently discovered have also been classified as dwarf planets. Even though there are many objects in the solar system, the solar system is mostly empty space. The distances between planets are so great that it would take many months just to reach Mars.

1. What does our solar system consist of?

Document 2

Many people from different countries have gone into space but only twelve people have walked on the moon. The moon is about 250,000 miles from Earth and the trip from Earth takes about three days. The first two people that walked on the moon, Neil Armstrong, and Dr. Buzz Aldrin made their historic walk in July

20th of 1969. Many people consider this event not only historic by heroic. No one knew what to expect when the LEM (Lunar Excursion Module) landed on the moon. Would there be deep dust that would make the ship sink, would the moon be so rocky that the ship would tip over as it landed? If the LEM landed, could the astronauts be able to leave the moon in the escape module? Other later manned trips to the moon included a lunar rover, a vehicle that allowed the astronauts the ability to travel further and to collect more lunar samples. There were six successful moon landings and a total of twelve people who have walked on the moon. It has been many years since the last man has walked on the moon but plans are in place to revisit the moon in the next decade.

1. How were humans able to travel on the moon?

Document 3

The following are some facts about several of the planets in our solar system. Mercury is so close to the sun that it is too hot to support us. Because of Mercury's rotation, a day on Mercury lasts nearly three earth months. Venus has upper level clouds that are poisonous sulfuric acid. Venus is much drier than Earth and its atmosphere is 90 times as dense and is composed of 96.5% carbon dioxide. Venus has no natural satellite (moon). Venus is the hottest planet, despite being further from the Sun than Mercury, with temperatures reaching more than 400 degrees Celsius. Mars possesses an atmosphere of carbon dioxide. Its surface shows that it was once geologically active and recent evidence suggests this may have been true until very recently.

The gas giant planets, so called because of their size and composition, are Jupiter and Saturn. Jupiter is 2.5 times the mass of all the other planets put together. Its composition of largely hydrogen and helium is not very different from that of the Sun, and the planet has been described as a "failed star". Saturn has many qualities in common with Jupiter. One of its moons, Titan is the only moon in the solar system with a substantial atmosphere, similar to that of the atmosphere of the early Earth. Uranus is the lightest of the outer planets. Unique among the planets, it orbits the Sun on its side. Uranus has 27 satellites. Neptune though slightly smaller than Uranus, is denser and more massive. Neptune has 13 moons. The largest, Triton, is geologically active, with geysers of liquid nitrogen, and is the only satellite to revolve around its host planet in a clockwise motion.

1. Describe two planets.

Document 4

The SUN is not a planet but is instead called a star. The largest component of the Sun is hydrogen. The Sun is greater than 800,000 miles across and the Sun's temperature is about 5,500°C. The Sun is classified as a moderately large yellow dwarf. The Sun is however rather large and bright. The Sun is growing increasingly bright as it ages. Early in its history it was about 75% as bright as it is today. The Sun is halfway through its life cycle and will eventually become larger, brighter, and redder until, about five billion years from now; it will become a red giant.

1. What is the Sun?

Document 5

Most comets are named after their discovers. Comets have orbits that zip past the sun, each at a frequency called a *period*. Most of the comets that we can see originated in a part of space called the Oort Cloud. A comet begins as a nucleus of frozen gases and dust less than a hundred kilometers across. When near the sun, its heated gas spread in a cloud like coma and stream away from the sun as a gas tail. Comets are usually found between the orbits of the inner planets and as far as beyond Pluto. There are two basic types of comet: short-period comets, with orbits less than 200 years, and long-period comets, with orbits lasting thousands of years. Some comets may originate outside our solar system. Old comets that have had most of their ices driven out by solar warming are often called asteroids.

1. Is Pluto a comet? Why?

Part B

For Part B, use the information from the documents, your answers in Part A, and your knowledge of our solar system to write a well-organized essay. In the essay, you should:

Write about our solar system.

For additional information on this topic the web site that I used was www. nineplantes.org

This exam was written to complement the student's geography lessons. It contains good information that can be found at the web site specified.

Assessment Exam 18—The Geology of the Earth—Earthquakes

This question is based on the accompanying documents (1-5). Some of the documents have been edited for the purpose of the question. The question is designed to test your ability to work with documents related to the geology of the earth and earthquakes. As you analyze the documents, take into account both the content of each document and any point of view that may be presented in the document.

Directions: Using the document, the answers to the questions in Part A, and your knowledge of our solar system, write, in Word, a well-organized essay about the geology of the earth. You should use a font of 14, font type of Times New Roman, margins of 1.25" for top and bottom, and 1" on both sides.

In your essay, remember to:
- Tell about earthquakes, what cases them and their effect on the earth.
- Include an introduction, body, and conclusion
- Include details, examples, or reasons in developing your ideas
- Use the information from the documents in your answer

Earthquake Background:

An earthquake is what happens when two blocks of the earth suddenly slip past one another. The surface where they slip is called the fault; the location below the earth's surface where the earthquake starts is called the hypocenter, and its location directly above it on the surface of the earth is called the epicenter. Although rare, moonquakes or "earthquakes" on the moon do occur. These moonquakes also are less severe than earthquakes. Some interesting facts about earthquakes include: from 1975-1995 there were only 4 states that did not have any earthquakes. They were: Florida, Iowa, North Dakota, and Wisconsin. Alaska is the most earthquake prone state. Alaska experiences a magnitude 7 earthquake almost every year, and a magnitude 8 or grater earthquake on average every 14 years.

Task:

For Part A, read each document carefully and answer the questions after each document. These answers will help you write your essay. Then read the directions for Part B and write your essay.

Part A
Short—Answer Questions

Directions: Read each document and answer the question or questions that follow each document by typing your answer in Word. *Be sure your name, grade and today's date are on the Word document.*

Document 1

The earth has four major layers: the inner core, outer core, mantle and crust. The crust and the top of the mantle make up a thin skin on the surface of the planet. This skin is not all in one piece—it is made up of many pieces covering the surface of the earth. These pieces, called tectonic plates, keep moving slowly around, sliding past one another and bumping into each other at tectonic plate boundaries. The plate boundaries are made up of many faults, and most of the earthquakes around the world occur on these faults. Since the edges of the plates are rough, they get stuck while the rest of the plate keeps moving. Finally, when the plate has moved far enough, the edges unstuck on one of the faults and there is an earthquake.

1. How do earthquakes occur?

Document 2

Scientists know when an earthquake has occurred because they use seismographs to record movement. The document below (The Global Seismographic Network (GSN)) indicates the many locations where seismographs are installed or planned to be installed. Many of the stations in and around the Pacific basin are part of the warning system that monitors earthquakes having the possibility of generating tsunamis (seismic sea waves). Seismic waves, recorded after they have traveled thousands of miles through the Earth's interior, bear significant information about the tectonic plates and the mantle and core that underline them. When the GSN is completed there will be a total of 128 stations in more than 80 countries on all continents. The GSN is the global complement to the U.S. National Seismographic Network (USNSN). GSN data allows scientists to understand why earthquakes of similar size differ greatly in their damage potential.

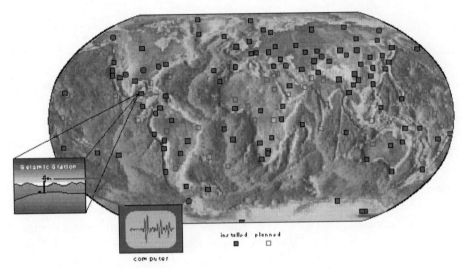

1. Explain how scientists can understand where earthquakes occur.

Document 3

It is estimated that there are 500,000 detectable earthquakes in the world each year; 100,000 of these can be felt, and 100 of them cause damage. Sometimes an earthquake has smaller foreshocks that occur before the mainshock or main earthquake. Mainshocks always have aftershocks that follow. These are usually smaller earthquakes that occur in the same place as the mainshock. Depending on the size of the mainshock, aftershocks can continue for weeks, months, and even years after the mainshock.

1. What is the difference between a *mainshock* and an *aftershock*?

Document 4

The San Francisco earthquake of 1906 was a major earthquake that struck off the northern California coast. The best guess at the strength of this earthquake was 7.8 magnitudes, a very large quake. Shaking was felt from Oregon to Los Angeles, and inland as far as central Nevada. The earthquake and resulting fire would be remembered as one of the worst natural disasters in U.S. history. Between 225,000 and 300,000 people were left homeless out of a population of about 410,000 and about 3,000 people died.

The earthquake and fire would leave a long-standing and significant impression on California. At the time of the disaster, San Francisco had been the ninth-largest city in the U.S. and the largest on the West Coast. Over a period of 60 years, the city had become the financial, trade, and cultural center of the West; operated the busiest port on the West Coast; and was the gateway to the Pacific, through which growing US economic and military power was projected into the Pacific and Asia. Over 80% of the city was destroyed by the earthquake and fire. Though San Francisco would rebuild quickly, the disaster would divert trade, industry and population growth south to Los Angeles, which during the 20th century would become the largest and most important urban area in the West.

1. What was a major result of the San Francisco earthquake?

Document 5

Sports games have been known to inadvertently produce small earthquakes. This was first seen in 1988 with the Earthquake Game at Louisiana State University, in which fans stamped their feet and jumped up and down enough to have the effect register on the campus seismograph.

Most large earthquakes are accompanied by other, smaller ones that can occur either before or after the main shock; these are called foreshocks and aftershocks, respectively. While almost all earthquakes have aftershocks, foreshocks occur in only about 10% of events. The power of an earthquake is always distributed over a significant area, but in large earthquakes, it can even spread over the entire planet.

1. What is the difference between a *foreshock* and an *aftershock*?

Part B

For Part B, use the information from the documents, your answers in Part A, and your knowledge of our solar system to write a well-organized essay. In the essay, you should:

> Write about the geology of the earth and earthquakes.

Additional information on this topic and other geology topics can be found at the U.S. Geological Survey web site www.geology.usgs.gov.

As a member of the IVHS (Intelligent Vehicle Highway System) committee and the ITS (Intelligent Transportation System), I know a lot about cars and highways of the future. The students of the seventh and eighth grade were already thinking about getting their first car and the combination of my knowledge and their interests lead me to create this exercise. I gathered several articles, which I felt the students were able to read, and gave them this exercise to work on at home. The fact that computers are now such a big part of car inventory and that will be even more so in the future made this an interesting exercise. You can prepare the same type of assignment by gathering several articles from automotive magazines.

Assignment 19—Cars of the Future and Computers

Cars of the future will use even more built-in computers than today. They will drive on highways that will also be safer. Cars will have accident avoidance systems and special lights similar to night vision goggles of today. They will be equipped with radar to help you in backing up and to avoid objects in the road. Cars will be semi-automated; they will drive on an automated highway at high speeds and at very close distance to other cars. They will be able to do this because of the many computer enhancements that will one day be available both for cars and for the automated highways of the future.

Your assignment is to:
- read the articles provided
- use any other articles or information you can find
- Write a report of at least one typed page explaining how computer enhanced cars of the future will work.

Please use a font of size 12, font Times New Roman, top and bottom margin of 1.1", both sides of 1.2"

Home Computer Assignment

Just about every one has at least one computer at home. In some instances, people might have several computers at home sharing devices such as printers. To give the students something that they could do at home, I created the following assignment. This assignment was used for the seventh and eight grades only. I gave them four weeks to work on the project. The intent of the assignment was to give them more experience with Paint and to give them some experience with networking. I did not expect them to actually install the equipment but rather to show where the equipment should go and why it should be installed in that room. If a student wanted a printer in the bathroom, I wanted to know why s(he) needed a printer in the bathroom.

Home Computer Assignment

If you do not have a computer at home, work on this assignment with another student.

- Draw a layout of your house (see below for an example) using Paint. If you have more than one floor in your house, you need to draw the floor plan for each floor. If you would rather use a made up floor plan you may do so. Do not show any furniture on the floor plan except what you need for the assignment.
- Decide where you will place computers and printers, fax machines, cameras, TV, and any other devices that you think you might need. You decide how many computers, etc you think you may need, BUT you need to justify why you are putting a computer in a specific room. The idea is to have equipment in your house perform some function. For example, maybe you want your computer on the first floor work as a security device with a camera attached to it. This camera could be setup to take pictures when activated.
- Layout your network of equipment and how it would be connected.
- You are not expected to know the actual connections but just what can be connected to what equipment. For example, can you attach a fax machine to a TV?
- You have four weeks to complete this assignment.

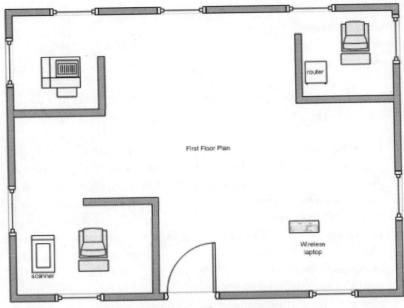

Figure 3—Floor Layout

Family Tree Project

This is another assignment that I used for the seventh and eight grades. The intent of the project was to give the students some experience with research, using the Internet, and some computer-drawing tool such as Paint.

For this assignment, I am asking you to investigate your family tree. You are to research, via the Internet, who your relatives are. You must go back at least to your great-great grandparents. You can start by questioning your parents. This will give you some idea of your four grandparents. From there you will probably need to research the next two generations. Note: I do not need you to find all your relatives, just a subset. Once you have done the research, you are to draw your family tree using some computer tool such as Paint. Examine the figure below to see how it should look. The drawing should include names and who they were. You can include brothers, sisters, etc.

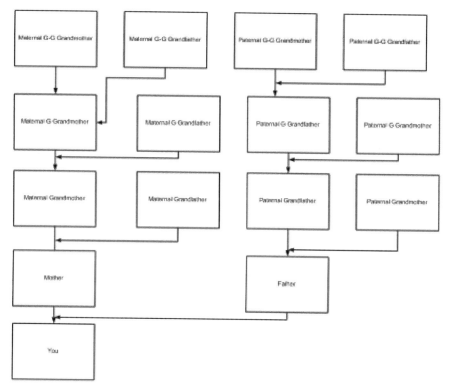

Figure 4—Family Tree

Web Project

This project was designed for the 7th and 8th grade students only. It is possible that some of the other students, such as fifth and sixth grade, could have performed most of the work on this project; I just was not convinced that it was a good idea to include them in the assignment. The basis of this project is; each class (7th and 8th grade) was to create a class web site. A class web site is not the same as a school web site. The class web site would be for the seventh or eight grade students only, whereas the school web site would include all grades in the school and would be much more comprehensive to design and write. The class web site was to be designed and created by the students as a team. This web site was to be designed and created by the students. I was available for help and trouble shooting but this was their assignment. The web site was to include, information about the school and clubs, a place for teachers to place assignments, e-mail for exchange of messages and any other thing the students felt should be placed in the web site. I asked the students to restrict pictures to those pertaining to the school and not to include pictures of themselves or other students. This requirement was given to me by the principal. She was concerned about possible legal issues pertaining to student pictures. Because I wanted the work done in class, I asked the students to create the web site using Microsoft Word.

In order to create a web site you can use one of the many good products on the market that can be used for this purpose. Some of these products include Macromedia DreamWeaver and Microsoft FrontPage. Because I did not want to teach new and complicated software in class, I decided to use Microsoft Word instead. Although Word adds lots of extra code (XML) which makes debugging more difficult, I decided to let the students use this software anyway because it was easy to use. The purpose of the assignment was for the students to have fun but also learn something new. The following diagram and instructions were used as the foundation of the web design project.

Class Web Site

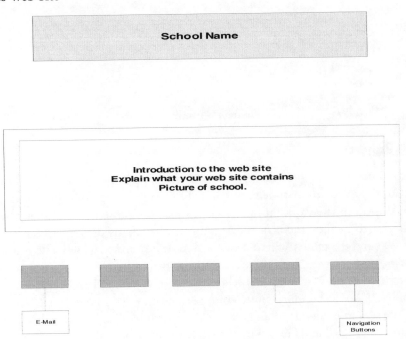

Figure 5—Home Page for Student Web Site

Instructions:

The following are the instructions that you should use to build your class web site. Remember, this is a class web site so you are working as a team with the other students to build this web site. If there is a difference of opinion, then the majority rules.

- Each navigation button should send the user to a new page.
- Each page should be one topic, such as the types of clubs or sports at the school.
- Include links on each page.
- Use the same buttons on each page.
- Be sure to include a home button on each page. The home button will send you back to the main menu.
- One button should be for e-mail.
- Do not include pictures of any students or yourself.
- If you have any questions, I am here to help

Notes:

- Try not to center text. Centered text is difficult to read.
- Make headings and subheadings bold and perhaps use a different font.
- Do not use more than two different fonts on a page. Multiple fonts make a page more difficult to read.
- Do not use blinking text or pictures. Blinking objects are distracting and are the sign of a novice programmer.
- If you use color backgrounds, etc., remember not all colors look the same on every type of machine.
- If you have more than two items in a list, use bullets.
- If you have a lot of text on the page, you should use short paragraphs and/or split the text into several pages.
- Do not fill the page, leave white space or you will overwhelm the visitor.
- Limit your picture size. Pictures can take a long time to download and people get impatient waiting for them.
- If you use a menu, do not use more than seven items in the menu.
- Do not use animation on your site because it is very distracting.

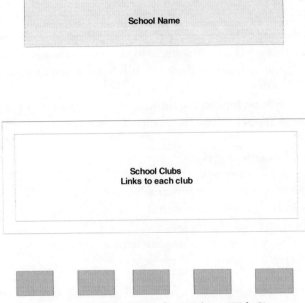

Figure 6—Sports Page for Students Web Site

When you are finished with the design, and it has been approved by the class and the teacher, then coding may begin. Coding is a fun experience that allows you to see how your design will look on a computer. Do not be surprised if what you see on the screen is not what you expected, this is very common in programming. It is just about impossible to code anything and get it right on even the third try. During the coding part of the project, you may find it easier to work together but have only one person do the typing. You should not work on this project alone or without supervision.

Web Project Information for Educators

Working with your senior students (grades 7-8) to develop a class or school web site can be an enjoyable project for both the students and the teachers. Creating a school web site can also bring legal issues as well as issues of security. Legal issues can arise when you include information obtained from another source (see *Installing Software*). Security issues can arise when you allow students and others to access the web site from outside the school. The following are a few guidelines that you may wish to use when creating your class or school web site.

Before starting this project, you need to answer some basic questions, such as:

- Do my students have the experience necessary to work on this project? Students can become frustrated when the assignment becomes too difficult for them. You need a firm understanding on what they can accomplish. At the very least, the students should have an understanding of: the Internet, what it is, what it is not, what it can be used for, and security issues related to the web. If they do not have this knowledge, it would be useful to use several periods giving them this information via class discussions and reading assignments.

- Students need to want to work on this project. If you have experienced students in your class, students who may have already created their own home page, you should use them as leaders for the project. Giving them this responsibility is an excellent teaching tool.

- How do you protect your web site from the misuse of a student making modifications? Once your web site is created and placed on the server you should restrict write access to the files. This can be done as the administrator, usually defined as the web master. The early version (test) of the web site should not be on the server but instead should reside on a local machine. This will make revisions easy to handle. Early designs will require many changes, from the background color to additional web pages. You and the students should not become frustrated with the changes; they are inevitable with any system. As with all programs and software, you should back-up your web site periodically.

- Does you school have the equipment necessary that would allow you and your students to build a web site? This includes the hardware, software, and Internet connection necessary to complete the project. The hardware should include a server that will be used to hold the web site software. The software should include whatever software you will use to create the web site as well as some firewall software. The firewall software will be used to restrict outside access to your web site. A firewall is necessary to protect the server from intruders who might be able to infect your system with a virus. If there is any form of Internet access available at your school, you should install firewall software or hardware. Virus protection software, if it is not already installed on the sever, should be installed and periodically updated.

- Should you include a school or class calendar? The calendar could let students know about important upcoming events. A calendar will also require constant updates. Do not include a calendar unless you are willing to change it frequently.

- Do you have the skills to work with the students on this project? Students today are very knowledgeable. In some cases, they may know more than the instructor knows, especially when it comes to the Internet and web development. If you lack the skills to work on this project, I suggest you do not start. The students will know soon enough that you lack the experience to help them.
- Should you include a web log or blog? A web log is similar to a digital diary. A blog can be used for students to place their reports for comments by other students. It is often used as an interactive publishing tool. A blog (the contraction of "Web log") is a website where entries are made in journal style and displayed in reverse chronological order. Blogs often provide commentary or news on a particular subject, such as food, politics, or local news; some function as more personal online diaries. A typical blog combines text, images, and links to other blogs, web pages, and other media related to a topic. Most blogs are primarily textual although some focus on photographs (photoblog), videos (vlog) or audio (podcasting), and are part of a wider network of social media. Since 2002, blogs have gained increasing notice and coverage for their role in breaking, shaping, and spinning news stories. Blogging by established politicians and political candidates cemented blogs' role as a news source. A good source of information on this new tool and how it can be used in the classroom can be found at www.weblogg-ed.com.
- How long will the project last and do you have the time? The design and coding of a school web site can be time consuming. Depending on how complex you want to make the site and the experience of the students, the project could last a semester. Can you dedicate this much time to a single assignment? You should also dedicate time for a discussion on the Internet, web design, etc.
- Should the assignment be for all the students or just the better students in class? Should the assignment be an after school assignment? Depending on the skills of your students, making the assignment a special after school project could be an effective alternative to an entire class assignment. Problems however could arise if the other students feel left out. One alternative could be to create a computer club and make the web site a club project.
- Why do you want to build a web site? This includes, what do you want the web site to do, to say, who will use it, etc. A web site can be used to share information between the teachers and the students. What information do you want to share and can you share it without a web site?

- What information do you want to make available to the students, the parents, other schools and people outside your school? At the least you should include:

a. Information about the school. This can include a picture of the school, location information, awards the school and students may have won, etc. You must be very careful if you want people outside your school to access the web site. If you post your pages where others can see them, people will find the site. What you post to the web site will be available for everyone to see, therefore you want to make the best impression for your school that you can.

b. You should include a page for teachers to place assignments. This could be one of the major benefits to having a school web site. By placing the assignments on-line, there cannot be any questions regarding what work the students are required to perform and when it is due. This is a great benefit if a student is out sick.

c. You should include a way for students and teachers to send mail to each other. Students love the idea that they can contact the teacher in this way. It gives them a sense of privacy. Teachers can use this feature to notify their class of upcoming trips or tests, as well as for student reminders.

d. You can include a page for school announcements. School announcements can include meeting notices, weather related announcements and special dates for people to be made aware. This page and the calendar could be combined into the same page.

- What software should you use to build the web site? Do you have the experience to code a web site or to help the students code a web site? Even if there are experienced students in your class, if you are not familiar with the software, you will not be able to help when the students experience trouble. There are many products available to use when building a web site. Many Internet providers, such as AOL, MSN and EarthLink, supply easy to use software that can be used to build a web site. Other software that you can use includes Microsoft Word, DreamWeaver, FrontPage, HTML, Java, and JavaScript. If you would like to use Word to build your web site, the following short discussion can give you a start on the project.

Using Microsoft Word to Create a Web Site

One of the easiest ways to create a web site is by using Microsoft Word; which is the product that my class used to create their web site. The following are some simple instructions that you can use to create your web site with Word.

First, select *File* then *New From Template* then *General Template* then *Web Pages* then *Web Page Wizard*. The Web Page Wizard will now have a series of questions for you to answer. With the Web Page Wizard you will be able to create a multi-page web site complete with navigation.

To create a web site using Word you should follow the next steps.
- The first page of the Wizard will allow you to create a title for your web site and a location to store your web site. While under construction, you should store the web site on a local disk. Word will create a file (suffix html) and a folder for each web page.
- The next Wizard screen will show you several screen layouts, some that use frames and at least one that does not use frames. Frames are a method for dividing the window into smaller sub-windows, each displaying a different document. Old browsers had a lot of difficulty with frames and in some cases did not support frames. Today, all versions of browsers support frames. Although frames are useful, especially for navigation, I do not use them on my own web pages because they do not display correctly if that page is linked to from another site that also uses frames.
- The next selection allows you to add pages to your web site. You can add blank pages, existing Word documents, or other web pages to your web site.
- The next selection will allow you to organize the navigation links to your web site.
- You can next add a visual theme to your web site. You may click on *Browse Themes* to examine the many themes available. You may not have all the displayed themes available in which case you will need to install the desired theme or use another theme that is already available.
- The next selection will just be a message that you are about to complete the web site. You should click the *Finish* button.

Hyperlinks are colored and underlined text or graphic that you click to go to a file, or location. Hyperlinks are very important in the design of a web site because you usually need to direct the reader to another place. Word makes it easy to insert hyperlinks to your page. To insert a hyperlink you just need to perform the next steps. First, click the *Insert Hyperlink* tool.

You can add many other complex designs to your web site with Word including; check boxes, text boxes, command button, option button, list box, combo box, toggle button and more. To add these tools you should select the type of insert you want from the tool menu. Adding these buttons will require some coding experience (VBA), because you need to code the action of the buttons. Once your web site is complete, you can see what it will look like on the web by selecting, *File* then *Web Page Preview*.

Building a class or school web site is a worthwhile project that can be used to teach your students many different skills. This project should be attempted, even if it is only a class web site that cannot be accessed from outside the school. You do not need a web provider to create a web site. A web site can be accessed as files from a server, without the use of AOL or any other provider.

REFERENCES FOR TEACHERS AND STUDENTS

The following books have proved useful to me in creating assignments and in developing class topics.

- Basic Mathematics, Rosanne Proga, PWS Publishing Company, Boston, MA, 1995

- The Birth of Writing, Robert Claiborne, 1974, Time Life Books,

- How the Future Began: Communications, Anthony Wilson, 1999

- Inventors and Inventions, Computers, David Wright, 1996

- The Parents Pocket Guide to Kids & Computers, Family Computer Workshop, 1998

- The Microchip Revolution, David J. Darling, Dillon Press, 1986

- Computers, Diane Gibson, Smart Apple Media, 2000

- Computer Simplified, IDG Books, 1998

- The First Computers by Charles A. Jortberg, Abdo & Daughters Press, 1997

- No-Stress Guide to the New York State 8th Grade Tests, Expert tips to help boost your score, Cynthia and Drew Johnson, Kaplan Books, New York, NY, 2000

- Robots A2Z, Thomas H. Metos, Julian Messer Press, NY, 1980

- Robotics Basics An Introduction for Young People, Karen Liptak, Prentice Hall, Englewood Cliffs, New Jersey, 1984

- Artificial Intelligence, Robotics and Machine Evolution, David Jefferfis, 1999, Crabtree Publishing, New York, NY

- Robots Machines in Man's Image, Isaac Asimov and Karen A. Frenkel, Harmony Books, New York, 1985

- The Story of Language, Mario Pei, New American Library,1949

- Dawn of Art: The Chauvet Cave, Jean-Marie Chauvet et al, 1996, Harry N Abrams, Inc. Publishers

- The Blue and the Gray, Thomas B. Allen, National Geographic Society, Washington D.C., 1992

- The Civil War An Illustrated History, Geoffrey C. Ward with Ric Burns and Ken Burns, Alfred A. Knop0f Inc, 1990

- Our Universe, Roy A. Gallant, 1980, National Geographic Society, Washington D.C

- Other Worlds—Images of the Cosmos From the Earth and Space, James Trefil, National Geographic Society, Washington D.C

I also found the following magazines helpful:

Technology and Learning. You can obtain a free subscription from: Technology and Learning Subscription Department PO Box 5052 Vandalia OH 45377-5052

WEB SITES FOR TEACHERS AND STUDENTS

By the time this book is published, there will probably be many more web sites for teachers and students to search. While documenting this book I discovered the following sites that may be useful for teachers.

- www.teachers.net—A site designed with teachers in mind.

- Cnets.iste.org/tssa—Technology standards for school administrators. This site is dedicated to developing technology standards for school administrators.

- www.ed.gov/poubs/EdTechGuide—an educator's guide to evaluating the use of technology in schools and classrooms.

- www.ncrel.org/sdrs/edtalk/toc.htm a site that offers links to a range of topics that can help in choosing and using educational technology.

- www.portical.org is the Technology Information Center for Administrative Leadership. This site is a portal for administrators.

Students will probably know more about the Internet and web sites than the teacher but the following web sites may be useful for specific topics and assignments.

- A+ Math www.aplusmath.com—a good site for math for ages 5-13.

- American memory http://lcweb2.loc.gov/ammem/ a treasure trove of artifacts from the library of congress converted into downloadable recordings, images and text.

- American Library Association http://www.ala.org/aasl/index.html

- Animal Tracks www.nwf.org/nwf/kids/index.html ages 5-12. This site from the National Wildlife Federation focuses on the land and animals of the U.S.

- AOL@School (school.aol.com) from AOL features six learning portals. Each portal delivers educational content and other services. This is a free service from AOL.

- Ask Dr. Math http://forum.swarthmore.edu/students This web site uses college math students to answer your math questions.

- B.J. Pinchbeck's Homework Helper tristate.pgh.net~pinch13 ages 7-13.

- Bedtime Story the-office.com/bedtime-story/ages 3-8. Possibly the biggest collection of children's stories on the Web.

- Britannica Internet Guide www.ebig.com for ages 9 –13+

- Children's Express www.ce.org ages 6-13, this web site is a news service produced by kids and covers issues that affect their lives.

- Commission on Online Child Protection (www.copacommission.org/papers provides shopping for research papers which analyze online safety issues and the pros and cons of filters.

- Computer History Museum www.computerhistory.org.

- Consortium for School Networking (www.safewiredschools.org) offers information on managing Internet content at your school.

- Dan's Wild Wild Weather Page www.whnt19.com/kidwx/ ages 6-13.

- This Day in History www.historychannel.com/today/ This site offers a thumbnail of each days history.

- Discovery Channel used in conjunction with the American Museum of Natural History. http://school.discovery.com/schooladventures/universe You can also go to the main page http://school.discovery.com to find other information.

- Disney Book Factory www.disney.com/DisneyBooks/ ages 3-11. This site offers fully illustrated storybooks to read on-line or print out.

- Encyclopedia.Com www.encyclopedia.com/home.html, ages 7-13. A good starting point for research.

- www.Techweb.com/encyclopedia/—a link to computer definitions

- Exploratorium www.exploratorium.edu ages 6-13. This site contains a world of scientific information.

- Extreme Science www.extremescience.com This Web site will take you to the outer limits of science, such as the highest stop on earth.

- Family History—Two sites that you can use to find out more about your family history are: www.usgenweb.org and www.ellisisland.org.

- Franklin Institute's Education Hotlists http://www.fi.edu/tfi/hotlists/index.html. A selection of sites for students to use to search for information.

- Getting started in Genealogy and family history (www.kbyu.org/ancestors) is a web site that can be used by students to build a family tree.

- Hubble Space Telescope—http://hubble.stsci.edu the official site for the Hubble Space Telescope.

- Human Genome project www.ornl.gov/hgmis

- Intel Innovation in Education web site at http://www97.intel.com/education/index.asp

- The Internet Public Library www.ipl.org/youth/ for all ages.

- The Jason Project www.jasonproject.org Follow actual scientists as they head out on scientific expeditions, communicate online.

- Kids Web www.npac.syr.edu/textbook/kidsweb/ for students in grades k-12. This web site offers links to art, science, weather and social studies sites.

- The Math Forum http://forum.swarthmore.edu a site for math education.

- Merriam-Webster www.m-w.com online dictionary and thesaurus.

- The Metropolitan Museum of Art for Kids ages 6-12 www.metmuseum. org/htmlfile/education/kid.html This site features many of the New York City Metropolitan Museum's possessions.

- Mister Rogers Neighborhood www.pbs.org/rogers/ ages 3-5.

- www.hplearningcenter.com sponsored by HP, these free courses include, Word, Excel, PageMaker, HTML and more.

- www.barnesandnoble.com This site offers free courses in beginning programming, graphics, and Web page design.

- www.electricteacher.com/tutorial2.htm This Web site provides step-by-step instructions on FrontPage tasks.

- www.Adobe.elementk.com This site contains information on Adobe PhotoShop.

- National Educational technology Standards www.cnets.iste.org

- www.memory.loc.gov/learn/lessons/index.html—this site lists about 70 lesson plans for teachers.

- www.microsoft.com/education/?ID=IOCTutorials This site contains tutorials on many Microsoft products.

- www.PBS.org/teachersource Teachers guides and development material.

- www.designer-info.com/index.htm This site offers a collection of free desktop publishing tutorials.

- Monster Math www.lifelong.com/CarnivalWorld/MonsterMath/ ages 3-7. This site use monsters who can't count to teach math.

- NASA www.nasa.gov NASA's main web site. You can see daily images from the Hubble Space Telescope.

- National Geographic Society Kids, ages 9-13. www.nationalgeographic. com/kids

- Natural History Museum www.nhm.ac.uk Displays at the London museum.

- Recommended Pre-K-12 Instructional technology Standards http:// www.doe.mass.edu/edtech/standards/itstand.pdf

- www.Sunsite.berkeley.edu/KidsClick is a web based search engine for kids.

- www.futurekids.com is one of the largest providers of classroom material about technology and the Internet.

- www.yahooligans.com is a kid friendly web search engine.

- www.searchoplis.com is a search engine as well as a Web index.

- www.internet-tips.net is web site that contains information on the Internet as well as a series of dos and don'ts of chatting on the web.

- www.collegeview.com allows you to take a virtual tour of many colleges on-line. You can also search for information on scholarships to those colleges.

- The Smithsonian Institute www.si.edu/resource/start.htm. You can enjoy exhibits from the Smithsonian including exhibits from the Air and Space Museum.

- www.techLearning.com is a resource for educators.

- Try Science www.tryscience.com. This web site brings you to a collection of 400 science centers from around the world.

- U.S. Fish and Wildlife Service www.fws.gov/r9endspp/Isppinfor.html. This is a general information site where you can learn about fish species.

- White House for Kids www.whitehouse.gov/WH/kids/html/home.html ages 6-13.

- The Why Files whyfiles.news.wisc.edu ages 9-13. The Why Files, funded by the National Science Foundation, deliver the science behind the news.

- Zoos and Aquariums around the world. http://now2000.com/kids/zoos.shtml Take a virtual tour of some zoos and aquariums from around the world.

- www.historychannel.com. This site is for history teachers and their students, upper-elementary through high school.

- History Link 101 www.historylink101.com. This resource contains links to many sites good for curriculum material. This site is good for upper-elementary and middle school students.

- The Encyclopedia of World History: Ancient, Medieval, and Modern www.bartleby.com/67. This site contains more than 20,000 entries spanning prehistoric times to the present. This site is good for grades 6 and higher.

- www.ciconline.org Cable in the Classroom

- www.jiwire.com/hotspot-locator-laptop.htm—a downloadable version of a hotspot locator.

- www.wikipedia.com—an online encyclopedia. Anyone can add entries to this site.

- www.portical.org—this portal, sponsored by the California and Arkansas departments of education, maintains a database of 400+ online resources for K-12 school administrators.

- www.Google.earth—a free system from Google that allows you to examine any part of the earth. There is also a Google.mars and a Google.moon web site.

These web sites can be used for history instructions:

World History, ABC-CLIO, www.abc-clio.com, grades k-12
Electronic Field Trips, Colonial Williamsburg Foundation, www.history.org, grades 4-8
Curriculum Pathways, SAS inSchool, www.sasinschool.com, grades 7-12

For those teachers whose students are in high school the following are several products and sites that can be used for SAT preparation.

- SAT QuizBank by Kaplan www.kaplan.com
- TestGear by Bridges Transitions www.testu.com
- Barrons Test Prep www.barronstestprep.com
- College Board www.collegeboard.com
- College PowerPrep www.powerprep.com
- Gorilla Test Prep www.gorillatestprep.com
- Harper Collins www.harpercollins.com
- Kaplan www.Kaplan.com
- Peterson's www.petersons.com
- McGraw-Hill www.mhlearningstore.com
- Sylvan Learning Centers www.educate.com
- The Study Hall www.studyhall.com
- Triumph College Admissions www.testprep.com

There may be times when a student needs more help than you or others can give. When this occurs it might be useful to consider an online tutor. Online tutors provide online, real-time, one-on-one tutoring in core subject areas over the Internet. Some online tutors include:

- Brainfuse, Trustforte Educational Services, www.brainfuse.com, 3-12 grade
- vTutor, Elluminate, Inc., www.elluminate.com/vtutor.jsp, 6-12 grade
- SMARTHINKING, SMARTHINKING, Inc., www.smarthinking.com, K-12 grade
- Tutor.com, Tutor.com, www.tutor.com, 4-12 grade
- eSylan, www.esylan.com, 3-9 grade

Several online tutors for teachers and students for computer topics are also available. These tutors, unlike the tutors listed above, do not use a real tutor but are self-driven where the student or teacher can learn at their own pace. These tutor products include:
- EasyTech, Learning.com, www.learning.com, k-8 grade
- Connected Tech, Classroom Connect, www.tech.classroom.com, k-8 grade
- Atomic Learning, Atomic Learning, www.AtomicLearning.com, 3rd grade to adult

SOFTWARE VENDERS AND SOFTWARE

The following is a list of some venders that sell educational software. The list is in no particular order. This list contains some titles that I have not examined.

- NetOp School by CrossTec Corporation. This is a network management tool that lets teachers control the display on each student's screen from one desktop location.
- Adobe Education (www.adobe.com/education)
- Bigchalk Library (www.bigchalk.com) is a student search page listed by student grades. You will find many interesting titles at this Web site. This firm is now part of ProQuest (www.il.proquest.com)
- Classwell Online by Classwell Learning Group.
- EasyTech by Learning.com.
- EBSCO Ultra Online Package provides students with a broad set of resources (www.epnet.com).
- Educational Insights (www.educationalinsights.com) provide the GeoSafari Phonics Lab.
- Horizon Software Systems (www.horizonss.com. This product line includes early childhood curriculum software among other things.
- KnowledgeBox by Pearson Broadband.
- Inspiration by Inspiration Software, Inc. This software, for grades 6-12, is a visual learning tool for students and teachers.
- IntelliTools (www.intellitools.com offers several software tools for classroom learning.
- JumpStart by Knowledge Adventure. Knowledge Adventure makes many titles including JumpStart Languages.
- LeapFrog SchoolHouse www.LeapFrogSchoolHouse.com offers PreK-8 curriculum and assessment programs.
- The Learning Company produces many titles including the Reader Rabbit series.
- LexisNexis Scholastic Edition is a national and international news source. (www.lexisnexis.com/academic/1univ/scholas/).

- Lightspan Reading Center by Lightspan. A reading center for K-3 grades.
- Disney produces many titles including Winnie the Pooh for Kindergarten.
- MindStorms by Lego. MindStorms is a series of robots that can be built and used in class.
- Concert by Pearson Education Technologies (www.PearsonEdTech.com) is a Web-based application for students, teachers, and parents.
- VideoStudio by Ulead is a program that captures digital video files from a camcorder.
- netTrekker (www.netTrekker.com) is a search engine for students and teachers.
- Riverdeep (www.riverdeep.net)
- SurfControl is an E-mail filtering software product.
- SAS in School produce many educational software products including Views and Voices: The Progressive Era.
- Soliloquy Learning (www.soliloquylearning.com) produce a reading assistant for grades 2-5.

INDEX

1274910